I0104665

LETS
GO
PUBLISH!

LETS GO United States of America!

Kill The Republican Party!

Bring on the American Party!

---Second Edition---

Replace the GOP with Americans for America.

In this second edition, we again emphasize that conservative Americans as well as nationalists, populists, as well as Americans for America need a party that we can count on. The elitist establishment Republican leadership is not doing it for us—by choice. This book describes the values of conservatives that are no longer important to Republicans. It offers a comprehensive rationale for why the Republican Party must be abandoned in favor of a brand new American Party. The American Party will be for all Americans.

Beware of the elite establishment Republicans as you would beware of wolves in sheep clothing, and in regard to them, the Ryan's, McCain's, Graham's, Rubio's, and McConnell's, invoke the old prayer: God protect me from my friends and I will take care of my enemies. Bring on the American Party!

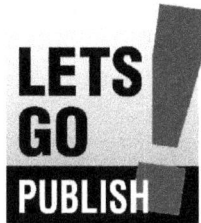

LETS GO PUBLISH

BRIAN W. KELLY

Copyright © 2014, 2016 Brian W. Kelly   Publisher/ Editor, Brian P. Kelly
Kill the Republican Party!   Author, Brian W. Kelly
Bring on American Party

Published by: LETS GO PUBLISH!
Publisher & Editor: Brian P. Kelly
Email: info@letsgopublish.com
                         www.letsgopublish.com

Library of Congress Copyright Information Pending
Book Cover Design by Michele Thomas, Editing by Brian P. Kelly

ISBN Information: The International Standard Book Number (ISBN) is a unique machine-readable identification number, which marks any book unmistakably. The ISBN is the clear standard in the book industry. 159 countries and territories are officially ISBN members. The Official ISBN For this book is on the outside cover:

The price for this work is :   **$9.99 USD**

10   9   8   7   6   5   4   3   2   1

Release Date: January 2014, August 2016

Dedication

I dedicate this book

To my wonderful children—Brian, Mike, and Katie.

We are a close family and my children help in every way they can to assure the muse is always fired up.

Thank you all!

Acknowledgments

In every book that I write or edit, I publicly acknowledged all of the help that I have received from many sources. Some of these wonderful people are still one earth and others have made their way to heaven.

I would like to thank many people for helping me in this effort.

I have listed their names and the story I usually tell on the Lets Go Publish! Web site-- www.letsgopublish.com. Look for the main menu. Please take a run out there and you will find the up to date text about all of those who are acknowledged for their help in bringing my books to you.

God bless them all

My plan is to update the acknowledgments on the LGP web site at least once every six months so that I can correct the names that are recorded wrongly, and add names that I have forgotten or who deserve credit for their new work.

Thank you all for all your help in keeping Lets Go Publish and our sales division BookHawkers.com (www.bookhawkers.com) on the top of the heap for so long.

As always, I must thank Nancy Lavan, our sponsor at Offset Paperback, our printer. She continually encourages us in our writing and publishing efforts. Arlene O'Malley, our customer service person from Offset at the time took over for stalwart Chris Grieves who is back on the job. Wiley Ky Eyely is also on the team. This team makes working with the printing process an easy task. Jozer Mickey (Joe McDonald) thinks this trio is the best! A special thanks goes to Michele Thomas, who still does these wonderful covers as a freelance cover designer. She takes ideas and makes wonderful images from them, such as this wonderful cover. She is a great talent. Dennis Grimes spent hours getting the book scans right. Thank you very much Bucko!

To sum up my acknowledgments, as I do in every book that I have written, I am compelled to offer that I am truly convinced that "the only thing one can do alone in life is fail." Thanks to my family, good friends, and a wonderful helping team, I am not alone.

Thank you all

Brian W. Kelly

Table of Contents

Preface:

Republicans have been AWOL during the Obama years for sure regarding matters of importance to conservatives. They blame conservatives for losing the Presidency in 2012, yet it was the Republican Party who put a semi-conservative up as its presidential nominee, not the conservatives. Though Mitt Romney was not a bad guy and would have made an OK president, he did have to look up the word *conservative* each time he gave a speech in order to reacquaint himself with conservative values.

It really does not matter at this point as it is almost a certainty that Republicans for some time now have been looking for a new base. Conservatives to them are passé. This book talks about the reasons why we conservatives should let them have their way. Let's go ahead and go it alone. Ironically while the Republicans were hoping the Hispanics would be their new base, Americans who love America decided that we would look for a candidate that the Republicans did not want. That man of course is Donald Trump.

This book asks conservatives to strongly consider pulling out of the Republican Party. The good ole boy elite establishment Republicans can learn to swim in their own complacency. America-lovers, conservatives and Tea Party people, who most often are one and the same, have a real enemy in the White House. His name as we well know is Barack Hussein Obama, and he has appointed his heir to be Hillary Rodham Clinton.

But, Obama is not just one person. He now has so many liberal progressive minions in so many government agencies from HUD to the EPA to Education, to Homeland Security etc. that if he were a good leader, he could have commanded this army of loyalists (if he knew how to command) into helping him take over the government all at once. Isn't that a frightful thought?

Obama has already issued the command to change the country fundamentally a little at a time, and his pace is speeding up. He does have to be somewhat concerned about moving too abruptly for if he is seen being cocky with his power, it would be a strategic mistake. That's why we still have some time to defeat him and all of his fascist and brainwashing propaganda and the programs he leaves behind. It is too bad that Republicans have chosen not to join conservatives in the fight.

There is a lot in this book about Obama, because he is currently American ultimate enemy # 1 of every conservative who ever lived. However, the intention of this book is to clearly demonstrate that the new Republican RINO leadership has willfully chosen not to fight Obama's most tyrannical moves on behalf of either themselves or conservatives. Obama is killing America and Republicans are acting as if they are enjoying being Obama's first casualties.

Why is this book about Republican leadership instead of the Democratic leadership? Democrats are always the clear and present danger. The answer hit me like a ton of bricks. It was a wake-up call. What seemed like out of nowhere, the GOP has chosen not to fight and not to help conservatives fight the many Obama messages and their armies of agencies.

It seems like a bad dream for conservatives when Republicans began to either believe they were dealt a winning hand in the Obama game or they were actually afraid of the President. Either way, these have been scary times for conservatives. Additionally, no reinforcements were coming any time soon from the Republican Party, who had already capitulated. Conservatives have to get accustomed to getting nothing from Republicans. We must go it alone. When Donald Trump showed up, we knew we had our leader.

For years, conservatives believed that the Republican Party's values and conservative values were the same. Conservatives do not have their own Party, and for many years or so it seemed, Republicans were the enforcers for the conservative ideology. Conservatives logically believed that Republicans felt the same as we do. We were wrong.

We all seemed to think during these Obama years that
Democrats and their fascist president have been ruining
America. We all seemed concerned about what Obama could do
in eight years, especially if he was able to convince Americans to
put in a House full of liberal progressives in 2014. Though it had
been brewing for a while, Republicans have clearly made a
decision to no longer represent even their own interests in
dealing with Democrats. There is no fight left in the Republican
Party for conservatives to rely upon. That is why most of us have
begun to look to Donald Trump as a last hope.

Conservatives, which make up more than 50% of the Republican
Party and a substantial portion of all other parties cannot afford
to sit around until there is no America and no freedom to defend.
We might joke about the prominence of Russia's Vladimir Putin
in today's world but as a leader he is not worse than Obama. He
is clearly for his country. Ironically Obama's foreign policy
permits the Chinese, the Russians, and rogue Middle Eastern
countries to continually make America look like a fool on the
world stage while our president bows and apologizes for our very
existence and our ability to sustain ourselves.

In the Economy and in foreign affairs, Obama has been killing us
and the Republicans have been pretending that "our day will
come," without any pushback to the Obama agenda.

In this book, we unabashedly recommend to stop trusting
Republicans since they have proven they will not fight for
America or for conservative values. The leaders of the Grand
Old Party have not even acknowledged that Obama and the
Democrats are wrong. Conservatives must go it alone.

The sooner conservatives cast off Republicans as our only
protection against Democrats, the sooner we can move on to
solving the problem for our values, our country, and our
freedom. We need our own Party for sure; for without a Party,
conservatives will not even be permitted to help on the battlefield
when America is hanging by just a thread. While we await the
right time to form a party, most of us think that we can defeat the

Democratic leadership, the corporations, the unions, the media, and the traitorous Republicans who are not worth the ground they stand on.

So we will all support Trump as a Republican. He will govern as a Republican, and while he is governing, we can work together to form The American Party, take all the little guys and leave the elite establishment to run their own party; take all the Democrats and Independents and members of other parties who love America. We can do it but let's get Trump elected first.

Brian W. Kelly monitors what is happening to conservatives and has written extensively on this major problem with the Republican Party. He is one of America's most outspoken and eloquent conservative spokesmen. He is the author of No Amnesty! No Way! Saving America The Trump Way, Why Trump? Taxation without Representation, Obama's Seven Deadly Sins, Kill the EPA! Jobs! Jobs! Jobs! and many other conservative patriotic books.

All Kelly books are now available at www.bookhawkers.com, Amazon.com, and Kindle. If they are not loaded up right now, they will be shortly. Like many Americans, Brian is fed up with a stifling progressive liberal agenda in Washington that places the needs of everybody else in front of the needs of Americans who love America. Like many conservatives, he is shocked at the behavior of the new RINO Republican Party.

Like you, Kelly is frustrated at how Republicans continually try to deceive conservatives so that we will believe they are still with US on values and policy. They want our votes but they no longer want to know what we think. It does not matter to these elites.

Brian Kelly has read the intelligence reports, has researched and written about the topic for years, and he knows how intolerable the results of poor government policy can be within our neighborhoods. His comprehensible and sane recommendations in this book are explained in detail within the covers of this soon-to-be classic book.

More and more Americans are clamoring for jobs but all that has been given by the President and his coterie is lip service. Republicans permit it. Americans want to keep their health insurance and pick their own doctors. Yet, Republicans, who can help change this for Americans have decided to cave to Democrats.

Obama is a fine politician and he would like nothing more than to be the dictator of America so that he does not have to abide by our Constitution and our American values. Unbelievable as it may seem, Republicans have decided to give him what he wants. Many Republicans have decided to give the same power to their choice for successor, Hillary Rodham Clinton.

In his eight years, Obama has tried to take away our guns; ram a health scam on Americans that includes death panels for the elderly and infirm; grant illegals citizenship while handing out American benefits, including free education; and finally permitting foreigners to take more and more American jobs. He just gave Iran $400 m in cash for 4 prisoners and he permitted them to grow nuclear bombs in their factories and he promised Americans would pay for their building.

Kill the Republican Party! has a major to-do in its title. In addition to showing why sucking up to RINO Republicans is bad for conservatives, Kelly also shows why it is bad for America and he tells us all what to do about it. You are going to love this book since it is designed by an American for Americans. Few books are a must-read but Kill the Republican Party has the prospects of ending the party of elites paid for by the US taxpayers.

Thanks to you, *Kill the Republican Party! Bring on the American Party!* (the 2016 version) is about to appear at the top of America's most read list.

Sincerely,

Brian P. Kelly, Editor

About the Author

Brian W. Kelly retired as an Assistant Professor in the Business Information Technology (BIT) program at Marywood University, where he also served as the IBM i and midrange systems technical advisor to the IT faculty. Kelly designed, developed, and taught many college and professional courses. He is also a contributing technical editor to a number of IT industry magazines, including "The Four Hundred" and "Four Hundred Guru" published by IT Jungle.

Kelly is a former IBM Senior Systems Engineer and he has been a candidate for US Congress and the US Senate from Pennsylvania. He has an active information technology consultancy. He is the author of 73 books and numerous articles about current IT topics and generally conservative thought. Kelly is a frequent speaker at COMMON, IBM conferences, and other technical conferences, & user group meetings across the US. Ask him to talk at your next TEA Party rally!

Over the past eight years, Brian Kelly has become one of America's most outspoken and eloquent conservative protagonists. Besides Kill the Republican Party; Kelly is also the author of *No Amnesty! No Way!*, *Taxation Without Representation*, *Obama's Seven Deadly Sins*, *Healthcare Accountability*, *Kill the EPA*, Jobs! Jobs! Jobs!, Saving America, RRR, Why Trump?, and many other conservative books.

Endorsed by the Independence Hall Tea Party in 2010, Kelly ran for Congress against a 13-term Democrat and, took no campaign contributions, spent enough to buy signs and T-shirts, and as a virtual unknown, he captured 17% of the vote—www.briankellyforcongress.com.

Chapter 1   Meaning of *Democrat* and *Republican* to Party Elites?

Are Party Labels Meaningful?

Americans need no more evidence that party labels are largely meaningless than what is happening right in front of them. Who is listening to the people? No Party is listening and no party is hearing the people of America. Democratic leadership refuse to use their ears. And, of course the newly "bipartisan" ruling establishment; influential members of the establishment wing of the GOP — neocons, warmongers, globalists, and so on hear nothing if it does not benefit them personally. What difference does a label make when opinions are already formed?

With Trump as the GOP heir of choice to the presidency, all of the above "establishment types," are checking out of the Republican Party, abandoning it, and in too many cases, they are jumping right on board the welcoming Democrat Hillary Clinton campaign saying *Damn the Republicans for Trump!*.

This cadre of miscreants are showing the true colors and allegiances they have hidden over the years. Regular American conservatives, populists, and nationalists, who had often looked to the Republican Party for values and overall goodness, even after many broken promises, have not been surprised to find the Republican establishment elites choosing self-interests over American interests. The game has not changed but today it is played in the open.

From the Bush war hawks who pushed Americans into war; to pretend conservatives; to the globalist hot shot members of the Council on Foreign Relations—even those like me from other Parties, looking for leadership from the Republican Party, have found nothing, and have concluded rightfully that there is nothing to find.

There once were the Republicans in Name Only (RINOs) siding with Democrats against the American people. Today they are emboldened enough to point blank offer that they are voting for Hillary Clinton. They have no problem proclaiming that the Republican candidate Donald Trump is unfit to serve. More specifically, they know he will not serve them and their selfish wants and needs. More than just a few of these globalist RINOs and neocon warmongers are now nestled in comfortable, well-padded seats, sipping their sweet Pina Coladas in the bar-cars on the Hillary Train.

Just take a look for a minute at the massive history book *Tragedy and Hope*, written by Bill Clinton mentor and establishment insider Carroll Quigley. In it, Quigley explains as succinctly and as pithily as can be, how American politics actually works in the real world. The real world is where those whose incomes do not come close to millions per year live and work. It is also the world in which the elite establishment believe their rule over political matters is absolute.

Quigley also explains that the benefits for those living outside the working class confines are so great for the elite that these insiders absolutely love it and simply do not care, nor have they really ever cared which party wins elections as long as they are members of the club of all important members, not the common folk. .

"The argument that the two parties should represent opposed ideals and policies, one, perhaps, of the Right and the other of the Left, is a foolish idea acceptable only to doctrinaire and academic thinkers,"

Quigley offers his conclusions with no emotion though it is huge news to most hoi polloi activists in both parties. He offers his own version of Nirvana: "Instead, the two parties should be almost identical, so that the American people can 'throw the rascals out' at any election without leading to any profound or extensive shifts in policy."

This explains why so many "important" Republicans seem to hate Donald Trump in so many unexplained ways. As far as the elitists in the establishment are concerned, Trump is a danger to the status as globalists, they are enjoying. Trump, with full support of real Americans who love America proudly slams the Hillary-backed Iraq and Libya wars and he blasts "globalism" as a threat to the interests of all Americans. Meanwhile Trump himself has emerged as the biggest threat to that whole "uniparty" idea.

There was a time when I thought that Rush Limbaugh had all the answers. Well, I think he has most but on the rationale for why the Republicans are falling off the Party Bandwagon in record numbers I had not heard Quigley's notion from Rush Limbaugh as of early August 2016. Yet, the smartest guy on why Trump has no big-time Republican player support now seems to be Alex Neuman, who is smart enough to quote a lot of Quigley when he offers his thoughts on the issue. I'd like to see what Rush Limbaugh thinks about this characterization!

Neuman hit a home run in his July 28, 2016 piece on thenewamerican.com web site. It is titled: "Neocons, *Warmongers, and Globalists Abandon GOP for Hillary.* It explains it all and it is a pretty disgusting thought for any American who wants America to continue to be America.

Neuman and Quigley immediately answer the question that conservatives have had since Republicans gained back the power in the House: "Why is nobody doing anything to stop Obama?" We have called Republicans names such as Wimps and RINOS and other unflattering terms as we watched them give it all up for Obama. After offering no fight, the RINOS gave the President all the budget money he needed to destroy our way of life. Quigley nailed it and Neuman blasts it out of the park with impunity.

The Republicans who run the Party do not care at all about the Party or the country. They do care about being cronies, warmongers, neocons, and globalists rather than being Americans. That's it. If America no longer offers them the big ticket items at a deal because of Trump, they are switching to Democrat, and many have done so already! That is how much these self-indulgent traitors care about having it their way.

The free press of course is bought and paid for by the Democratic Party and thus it is not really free and thus it no longer serves as the fourth estate. Every now and then the press may get it right but by accident. My great friend Dennis Grimes loves to say, "Even a blind squirrel finds a nut once in a while." Neuman writes:

"Ironically, establishment media outlets are touting the establishment GOP defections to Hillary among neocons and globalists in an apparent effort to hurt the Trump campaign. Apparently, they are oblivious to the fact that the defections of widely loathed establishment warmongers from Republican ranks actually bolsters Trump's arguments of a "rigged" system — not to mention his credibility in the eyes of supporters on both sides of the political spectrum, including among embattled "working class voters" and union members long considered reliable Democrats.

"Recent polls make that clear, with Trump's campaign surging ahead of Clinton's and attracting hordes of disaffected Democrats opposed to globalist "free trade" deals and endless wars."

"One of the many leftist media outlets celebrating the anti-Trump RINOs is the Daily Beast, a sort of wannabe establishment outlet that is unabashedly left-wing. The Beast compiled a list of some

of the "biggest GOP names" backing Hillary Clinton so far."
[We present this and more late in this chapter.]

"According to an alleged "source" within the Clinton camp,
"highlighting Republicans who've crossed over will be a key
fixture in campaign ads this fall." If the list provided is
representative of those "Republicans" to be highlighted, though,
Clinton better hope Americans have a short memory. Indeed,
aside from some no-name lobbyists and bureaucrats, the list is
practically a who's who of the most politically toxic
establishment globalists, banksters, and neocons on the planet."

"Consider: At the top of the list of prominent alleged
Republicans pushing Clinton is globalist bankster Henry "Hank"
Paulson. Among other supposed accomplishments, the Goldman
Sachs CEO and George W. Bush Treasury secretary helped
oversee the redistribution of trillions of dollars in public money
from middle class and poor Americans to billionaire Wall Street
insiders. According to lawmakers, they were threatened by
Paulson and his cronies with a declaration of martial law if
Congress refused to approve the "banker bailout" heist. Now,
Paulson spends much of his time pushing the discredited man-
made global-warming theory hoping to profit from the radical
policy schemes."

"Also featuring prominently on the list are many of the neocons
responsible for squandering trillions of tax dollars and hundreds
of thousands of lives — if not millions — on undeclared, illegal
wars based on lies. Chief among them is neocon Robert Kagan, a
senior fellow at the far-left globalist "think tank" Brookings
Institution and a co-founder of the fringe Project for the New
American Century that helped lead America into Iraq under
Bush. Aside from his own non-stop warmongering seeking to
send your children off to die in undeclared wars, Kagan is
married to senior Obama official and fellow warmonger Victoria
Nuland. Naturally, Kagan is on Team Hillary."

"Another senior neocon globalist on the Hillary Train is Max Boot, a left-wing Council on Foreign Relations (CFR) operative who claims to have been a "lifelong Republican" despite his love for Big Government. "[Hillary Clinton] would be vastly preferable to Trump," Boot was quoted as saying, adding that he hopes the GOP will split. "What she basically espouses is a pretty mainstream view." Of course, what Clinton espouses is so far from mainstream, it's hard to believe anyone, including fringe neocons, actually believes something so ridiculous. Just a few days ago, a poll showed eight in 10 voters want more restrictions on abortion, while Clinton wants even less restrictions and more tax funding for it. Almost no Americans except Hillary Clinton, the DNC, and fringe abortion activists support any tax funding for abortions. And that is just the start"

Thank you Mr. Neuman

Why are so many big shots breaking off the Republican bandwagon in the light of day? First of all; it is because they think it is safe to do so. They don't see themselves getting hurt because a good number of their cronies are doing the same thing. It is also because they have always been self-first and now that Trump threatens their comfortable way of life, they find jumping the Republican Ship as a way to protect themselves

The biggest mass exodus from anything that anybody has seen so far, however, is the exodus of pure conservatives from being just conservatives to becoming populists and nationalists. Donald Trump has actually taught us all that what has really been aggravating us about the stodgy elitists in the GOP, especially recently, is that we are Americans for America, and they are selfish louts out for themselves. We had never gotten the message that patriotism was dead.

We the people see Trump's presidential campaign and his nomination as the birth of a new American right, that is built on a strong desire to feel good again about America. It is based upon a sense of nationalism and populism that has always been there but may have been buried somewhere in our conservatism.

No longer are conservatives fully ideologically pure, and that is OK because nobody of whom I am aware at the grassroots level, where I live, is moving from conservative to liberal or progressive or Marxist. We are looking for goodness in leadership to bring us a great future. We think Donald Trump is that leader!

I listen to Limbaugh every day for three hours, except for the time from 12 to 3 that I doze off as it is nap time for all sixty-eight year olds. Nationalism and populism have clearly overtaken conservatism in terms of appeal," Limbaugh has been saying this quite often recently. He is right on the mark.

Rush Limbaugh well understands that many voters are simply "fed up" with the Democratic Party and have been for quite a while. They had been patient with Republicans for years but saw no action coupled with a new and obvious disdain for the masses. And, so now, we the people have become angry with Republicans in Congress, and we simply no longer trust them with our political fate.

We are angry with those who provide no real opposition in Washington. Who is supposed to take on the Democrats and Obama if not Republicans? Hopefully, the actions of elitist establishment Republicans will not mean that we get Hillary for eight years after Obama.

We the unwashed masses are the new-nationalists and populists while we are still mostly conservative. We have all fallen for the idea that we might be able to fall in love with Al Jolson's America again as we can play his old songs in a happier America. You see, with Trump, it is not pure conservatism that is uniting us or motivating us. It is America.

Until Trump came along, none of us were really sure. That's what everybody has been missing in Washington and throughout the country. American conservatives have found a way to bring back our America and it is not by being staunch Republicans. It is by following Donald Trump into battle and winning the day for America and Americans and our pre-Obama way of life.

We see Obama as the anti-American and Hillary as the same. Donald Trump is our Captain America. He is a phenomenon and history will record him as such. My friends and I are very glad he is in the race.

Everything Obama and Hillary stand for, we are against. It is axiomatic. We are in direct opposition to the left, to the Democratic Party, to Obama, to Hillary, and everything that's been going on for the last seven to eight years. We are mad as hell and we want it stopped and reversed. We really will go anywhere if we are convinced whoever's telling us they're gonna stop it is telling us the truth. We believe that man today, a unique truth-teller in an era of lies, is Donald Trump.

We like Trump as much for the fact that we do not perceive him as part of the establishment as we do for his simple solutions that are best for the country. Even if the solutions are difficult to achieve, we admire Donald Trump for having the moxie to get on the ball-field and do his best to win the game. We believe in his ability to make us all winners. There will be no losses and no losers on the Trump team.

Rush Limbaugh knows that Americans are angry at "Republican establishment central" in Washington. Donald Trump shares our anger and disdain for *Establishment Central*, and we love him for that.

Limbaugh believes that the new Nationalists and Populists are not necessarily committed as much to the conservative orthodoxy, especially when it comes to abstract principles or free market economics. For me, I have always been America-first but nobody other than Donald Trump has capitalized on that notion. And so, as a conservative, I have no problem being a Nationalist and a Populist. I want America to survive and have a great future.

"They don't have to be conservative," Trump explained. "They don't even have to be Republican." As a Democrat myself, I found that refreshing.

Indeed, Limbaugh argued the formation of the Trump coalition shows conservative ideology is relatively unimportant when it comes to creating conservative voters. None of that matters as Obama and Hillary will destroy America before we even know it is being attacked.

On a recent show, Limbaugh read from a 1996 article in the magazine Chronicles titled "From Household to Nation," authored by the late Sam Francis.

He was discussing populism and nationalism when he quoted Sam Francis from this 1996 article. Here is the quote:

"Sooner or later, as the globalist elites seek to drag the country into conflicts and global commitments, preside over the economic pastoralization of the United States, manage the delegitimization of our own culture, and the dispossession of our people, and disregard or diminish our national interests and national sovereignty, a nationalist reaction is almost inevitable and will probably assume populist form when it arrives.

When Francis was writing this piece in 1996, he was talking about a rogue Patrick Buchanan presidential campaigns. Francis had served as an adviser to the campaign. Ironically, though Buchanan is unquestionably one of America's great ones, Francis's prognostication can be brought into the present and just about all he wrote applies to Donald Trump. One can see in Francis's writings that he was predicting the rise of Trump.

We all know that Trump's signature issues are opposition to illegal immigration and opposition to bad trade deals against American interests. Trump is not just a man that gets our nationalist pro-American juices going, he has the ideas necessary to do the right thing even though the donor class is against it.

That is why so many of the establishment elites are against Donald Trump and why the people who learn who he is are so dedicated to his victory. Government hates him. Elitist establishment Democrats and Republicans hate him. Union bosses hate him yet their members love him. Corporations hate him, and of course the corrupt media, a branch of the Democratic Party also hate Trump. Only real people—my neighbors and your neighbors like Trump because he will create an America for us, not for the donor class to count their increasing wealth,

That means CNN. MSNBC, ABC, NBC, and CBS all hate Trump and unfortunately for conservatives, half of the bigshots on Fox openly hate trump. Again, that is a big reason why the people love him. Those guys that we love to hate; hate Trump.

In days past, even the Robber Barons cared about America while they cared about their wealth. They were not at odds with the country. Today it seems our culture has given the big and the powerful the right to enjoy their riches selfishly and not to worry about anybody else—even their country.

Today as I was at Mass, I heard a great homily. The Priest talked about rich people who love their money more than anything else. It made me think of the elite establishment in both political Parties. No time to worry about anybody else while collecting all their gains and fixing elections with their available cash.

St. Anthony of Padua has a big heart and in one of his sermon at the death bed of a rich man, he suggested that the dead man's remains had everything but a heart. His heart was not with the poor or the needy or with those he should have loved, but instead, Anthony told the crowd at the funeral that this man's heart was buried with his treasure, and it was not with his body. He asked the participants in the funeral to go ahead and see for themselves. This is the story:

"In a few words, on true and false love, [St. Anthony] preached at the funeral of the Florentine notable! Anthony's text was: "Where thy treasure is there thy heart is also." Pausing suddenly, he beheld in a vision the soul of that rich man in torment. He exclaimed: "This rich man is dead and his soul is in torture! Go open his coffers and you will find his heart." The astonished relatives and friends hastened to do his bidding; and there, half buried among the gold pieces, they found the still palpitating heart of the dead Croesus."

The good news today is that a billionaire such as Donald Trump with a heart and with a lot of love for family, friends and country is ready to serve America. We the people need Donald Trump more than he needs us. He is one of a kind. Let's elect him.

Big time billionaire Meg Whitman, who has been trying to win elections as a Republican for years but nobody wants her is currently the CEO of HP. Maybe she bought her way into the job. All I know is she has no loyalty to HP or to her Party, the Republican Party. She made the news recently for abandoning the Republican Party because of its support for Donald Trump. Whitman is going "D." She is going all out for Hillary Clinton. She said she would donate as much as she could to Hillary. Of course Whitman knows that if Trump, a man for the people is elected, her wealth will not increase. But, if Hillary, a broker for the status quo in which rich Meg can get richer, is elected President then Whitman's heart will be surrounded by lots more gold and treasures in her coffers as it beats for eternity without her body and soul.

Talking about a traitor. But, maybe not! Maybe Whitman never, ever, was a conservative. When trying to be elected, maybe she was faking us all; maybe she would have kept up the fake and she might have tried to run again for Republican President if she did not think Trump was going to win this time.

Maybe Trump is bringing out the truth in a lot of stodgy old billionaires, male and female, such as Meg Whitman, along with big-time "R" donors, who demand their pound of flesh from America. We won't be seeing them in the American Legion or in the VFW any time soon anyway, as they stay clear of the great unwashed masses. But, I think we will begin to see a guy like Donald Trump—a real American—at American Legions and VFW's across the land. Don't you think? Where will you find Meg Whitman? Look up the word, "posh."

A caller on the Rush Limbaugh show this past week put the Meg Whitman deal in perspective. As CEO of HP, she cares about corporate profits before she has any thoughts on America and Americans. The caller discussed what he called a secret policy at HP that was to assure 70% of American jobs with HP would be gone.

The jobs would be offshored so the corporation could make more money. So, one would think that in addition to union workers, the corporate employees and retirees who learn about their company CEOs being anti-Trump, will become Trump guys like many of us. He has an anti-off-shoring stance. No regular American who worked for an offshoring type of corporation, ever begged the corporation to ship out even more jobs. These folks will be pressed to vote for Trump to protect American jobs.

We all know some big names like the three Bushes, Romney, Whitman, and others who have gotten on the *Never Trump* bandwagon. I wonder who they expect to appoint the next Supreme Court Nominees—Hillary Rodham Clinton? Let's remember these names listed below and remember that they let us all down by playing for the other team. Do not elect them for dogcatcher and if you can buy a product from another company than from one, whose CEO is against Trump, please do so.

A list of others, traitorous Republicans, who have disgraced their own Party and who have abandoned their nominee, Donald Trump, who may or may not be on the list of disgraced "Republican" neocons, globalists, and establishment insiders but

who are fully pushing a Clinton presidency, include the
following names. Don't ever forget them!"

- ✓ Ken Adelman
- ✓ Rep. Justin Amash, R-Mich.
- ✓ Richard Armitage
- ✓ Gov. Charlie Baker, R-Mass.
- ✓ Brian Bartlett (Romney)
- ✓ Glenn Beck
- ✓ Michael Berry
- ✓ Max Boot (Rubio)
- ✓ George Bush the Elder
- ✓ George W. Bush
- ✓ Jeb Bush
- ✓ Sally Bradshaw
- ✓ Bruce Carroll,
- ✓ Jay Caruso, RedState
- ✓ Mona Charen,
- ✓ Linda Chavez
- ✓ Dean Clancy
- ✓ Eliot Cohen (Bush)
- ✓ Sen. Norm Coleman, R-Minn.
- ✓ Maria Comella
- ✓ Charles C. W. Cooke
- ✓ Doug Coon
- ✓ Rory Cooper
- ✓ Jim Cunneen
- ✓ Rep. Carlos Curbelo, R-Fla.
- ✓ Steve Deace
- ✓ Rep. Bob Dold, R-Ill.
- ✓ Erick Erickson
- ✓ Mindy Finn
- ✓ Tony Fratto
- ✓ David French
- ✓ Jon Gabriel
- ✓ Sen. Lindsey Graham, R-S.C.

- ✓ Michael Graham
- ✓ Jonah Goldberg
- ✓ Alan Goldsmith
- ✓ Stephen Gutowski
- ✓ Rep. Richard Hanna, R-N.Y
- ✓ Jamie Brown Hantman
- ✓ Stephen Hayes,
- ✓ Doug Heye
- ✓ Quin Hillyer
- ✓ Ben Howe,
- ✓ Brit Hume (Fox)
- ✓ Rep. Bob Inglis, R-S.C.
- ✓ Cheri Jacobus
- ✓ Robert Kagan
- ✓ John Kasich
- ✓ Randy Kendrick (big donor)
- ✓ Matt Kibbe
- ✓ Rep. Adam Kinzinger, R-Ill.
- ✓ Philip Klein
- ✓ Charles Krauthamme (Fox)
- ✓ Bill Kristol
- ✓ Mark Levin
- ✓ Justin LoFranco (Walker)
- ✓ Kevin Madden (Romney)
- ✓ Bethany Mandel
- ✓ Tucker Martin
- ✓ Gov. Bob McDonnell's, R-Va.
- ✓ Mel Martínez (RNC)
- ✓ Liz Mair
- ✓ Lachlan Markey
- ✓ David McIntosh
- ✓ Dan McLaughlin
- ✓ Ken Mehlman (RNC)
- ✓ Tim Miller
- ✓ Joyce Mulliken
- ✓ Ted Newton (Romney)
- ✓ James Nuzzo
- ✓ Katie Packer
- ✓ Gov. George Pataki, R-N.Y.
- ✓ Henry "Hank" Paulson

✓ Rep. Ron Paul, R-Texas
✓ Katie Pavlich
✓ Brittany Pounders
✓ Rep. Reid Ribble, R- Wisc.
✓ Ricketts family, (GOP mega-donors)
✓ Gov. Tom Ridge, R-Pa.
✓ Rep. Scott Rigell, R-Va.
✓ Mitt Romney
✓ Paul Rosenzweig
✓ Karl Rove
✓ Jennifer Rubin
✓ Patrick Ruffini
✓ Sarah Rumpf
✓ Mark Salter
✓ Rep. Mark Sanford, R-S.C.
✓ Sen. Ben Sasse, R- Neb.
✓ Elliott Schwartz
✓ Gabriel Schoenfeld
✓ Tara Setmayer
✓ Ben Shapiro,
✓ Evan Siegfried
✓ Ben Stein
✓ Alan Steinberg
✓ Brendan Steinhauser
✓ Stuart Stevens (Romney)
✓ Paul Singer (GOP donor)
✓ Erik Soderstrom (Fiorina)
✓ Charlie Sykes
✓ Brad Thor
✓ Senator Pat Toomey (R-PA)
✓ Michael R. Treiser (Romney)
✓ Daniel P. Vajdich (Cruz)
✓ Connor Walsh (Cantor)
✓ Rep. J.C. Watts, R-Okla.
✓ Peter Wehner
✓ Gov. Christine Todd Whitman, R-N.J.
✓ Meg Whitman (HP)

- ✓ George Will,
- ✓ Rick Wilson, Nathan Wurtzel
- ✓ Bill Yarbrough
- ✓ Dave Yost

That's not all and there will be more. Washington insiders are threatened that Donald Trump, one of the few good guys out there may take the gravy train right from their mouths. These people are lobbyists or are taking the money of lobbyists to undermine the American people. It actually proves Trump's point that he is the non-establishment candidate. He is and American for America and those traitor Republicans are why he deserves to be elected. I would be disappointed if they liked him.

The good news for America, another fifty came out of hiding on August 8, 2016 just intime to help Trump get a bounce from his great economic speech. Yes, fifty prominent Republican foreign policy and national security experts -- many veterans of George W. Bush's administration—aka Elite Establishment Republicans signed a letter denouncing Donald Trump's presidential candidacy and pledging not to vote for him. They are simply traitors and they still think they own the Republican Party. Well, there money will not buy the people anymore.

The letter includes the ultimate slam: "We are convinced that in the Oval Office, he would be the most reckless President in American history." These are all Bushies and because Jeb got his poor little feelings hurt when he spent over 100 million and Trump spent nothing and Jeb could not get more than 5% of the vote, he had to blame somebody. So, he blamed Trump, the guy who beat him.

Now, the Jeb Bush loyalists—all elite Republicans and members of clubs which have policies to keep you and I from ever getting close to their parking lots, hoping to protect their lobbyist cash, have decided to try to fool Americans by attempting to sully Trump's reputation. Good luck. By the way thanks for coming out as anti-Republican. You are why

Republicans lose elections. You are all worthless traitors who find more value in Hillary Cinton than the man Republican voters chose as the nominee of what was once your Party.

Besides the group above, you know who you are. Your names are on the nasty letter. I am talking about all those who have been dependent on the Bush machine over the yeats including former CIA and National Security Agency Director Michael Hayden, former Director of National Intelligence and Deputy Secretary of State John Negroponte and Eric Edelman, who was Vice President Dick Cheney's national security adviser and has worked closely with Michele Flournoy -- a candidate for secretary of defense in a prospective Clinton administration -- to forge a centrist group of defense experts on key military issues.

The newly announced traitors also include two Homeland Security secretaries under Bush, Tom Ridge and Michael Chertoff, and Robert Zoellick, a former World Bank president, U.S. trade representative and deputy secretary of state.

These guys are such big shots, the doors in their homes had to be widened just to help get their big heads in. Trump's campaign responded appropriately to the traitors with a statement from Trump denouncing the signatories as the very people who deserve the "blame for making the world such a dangerous place." Amen!

When Republican non-elites (folks like you and i) have the great sense to no longer cling to a party that has abandoned them, this new notion of which I speak, the American Party will save its day. Meanwhile, those Republicans who chose to abandon the party, with a partial list shown above, will rue the day. Why would one of us ever give them an opportunity for anything in the future after that have plotted and almost destroyed our county?

God Bless America a million zillion times. We all need it!

Chapter 2   Wimpy Republicans Have Already Killed the Party

The 2016 Party of Wimps

Let the Republican leadership and the elitist conservatives in the shadows stand down.

When I was contemplating revising this book that I originally wrote three years ago, I acknowledged to my conservative friends my plans for a new book. This was my forty-ninth book. I write fast.

At the time, I had yet to write a word for this book, but I knew the words would flow. I was beginning to burn inside because of wimpy, gutless Republicans, who no longer stand for anything and no longer stand up for anything. How much is a conservative supposed to take?

So, among other things, I started trying to figure out just how long the Republicans been playing lap dog for the Democrats? I remember many disappointments over the years.

I am sure it is more than twenty years ago and probably more than thirty that this phenomenon began. Conservatives have been far too patient, rooting for a Party that no longer has respect for even itself.

You probably did not believe how many conservatives had become upset with Republicans, and you probably did not believe how many use the same exact term—"wimps," to describe the Republicans of today. Then, along came Trump, just as in the 1950's when the song *Along Came Jones was* determined to make everything right again. You may know that this fabulous song, *Along Came Jones* was recorded on March 26, 1959 by the Coasters and released in May 1959. They sure were great days in America. Back then, fun was permitted.

Wimp is the right word for the elitist Republicans of today for sure. Here is a definition for WIMP: a weak and cowardly or unadventurous person. Yes sir! We sure have picked the right word. Indeed! Well, since most of you reading this book are conservatives, I suspect you believe it and you are not surprised.

I hope you enjoy the beginning of this article from 1994 titled, "Wimpy Republicans." It is nice to have our conclusions affirmed and this article does that and more. If we substituted the gang of eight amnesty charade for the crime bill in this article, it would sound like it was written just a few years ago.

"Wimpy Republicans"   September 09, 1994 by Mona Charen from the Baltimore Sun

"THE CAPITULATION of six frightened, feeble, supine Republican senators on the so-called crime bill does not bode well for the debate over [Hillary's] health care legislation. It suggests that some Republicans are still playing by rules invented by and for Democrats. If those rules are followed on health, we will get some kind of reform bill -- and that will be terrible for the country and politically damaging for Republicans as well.

The rules that were followed on the crime bill are as follows: The Democrats propose a huge federal spending program to address a problem that ought not to be handled by the federal government in the first place. The Republicans complain about the cost. The Democrats accuse the Republicans of being "anti-elderly" or "anti-children." Republicans stammer in response. The Democrats make some minor adjustments to the act (like cutting $3 billion from the $33 billion crime bill), and the Republicans vote for it."

The more things change, the more they stay the same. I found the scenario similar to today and utterly amazing that this has been going on for so long that few can remember when Republicans had guts.

On December 11, 2011, Republicans were at it again. Here is a part of a piece from conservativeviewsforthegrassroots.com:

"Republicans caved under pressure. ... though a two month extension won't solve things in the long term, it will help temporarily to give the 2 million people out of work some reprieve and spare doctors from a big Medicare cut. This will save each tax payer $40 per paycheck. This is called deferring the battle for another day. In other words, Congress is being stupid. A two-month extension only perpetuates the uncertainty that too many employers already have in dealing with the economy and what's coming out of Washington. Prolonging the agony will not suffice the American people."

Conservatives have been begging Republicans to do their jobs for an awful long time. They have quietly refused. Now that Donald Trump and the people demand that they do their jobs, they find it more convenient to attack Donald Trump and the people.

On May 7, 2013, in Virginia, the state Republicans chose to emulate Capitol Hill. This excerpt is from beforeitsnews.com:

"Remember that commercial for trash-bags; the one that describes their competitors trash-bags as wimpy, wimpy, wimpy. When I see other states and their reaction to the Federal government on the 2nd Amendment and other issues; that "wimpy, wimpy, wimpy" phrase perfectly describes your GOP legislators in Virginia.

Bob Marshall's exceptionally weak 2nd Amendment protection bill couldn't even make it out of a committee as GOP lawmakers wrung their hands that they might offend their "friends" in Washington. While Virginia Republicans cower and shake, other states are standing up for their citizens' rights."

On December 3, 2012, Michael Reagan made some astute observations about the GOP:

"Republicans had better learn from history -- and from Ronald Reagan's mistake.

President Obama and his fellow big-spenders in Congress are promising if they get higher tax rates today they'll make even higher spending cuts tomorrow.

It's an old sucker's game. Republicans -- and the rest of the country -- should know it by now, because for three decades we've all been suckers.

If history is our guide, and Republicans in Congress don't grow a spine, by this time next year we'll have higher taxes, higher spending, more debt and a bigger government."

At renewamerica.com on May 14, 2011, Bill Borst took an extended look at the Republican Wimp Factor:

"...**Newsweek** was saying that Republicans were too nice...or maybe too civil.

"What has become a catch phrase for President Obama has been historically a vice for Republicans, and a certain formula for political defeat. Democrats believe Republicans are so wimpy that they counsel them on how to behave.

"President Obama thinks because of Indiana Governor Mitch Daniels' intelligence, he would make a formidable opponent who could beat him in 2012.

"And the Yankees let the Red Sox pick their starting pitchers!

"Many Republicans will probably fall for this Obama trap. Most Republicans have been overly solicitous in their appearance of civility and political restraint. It was true of H.W. and also W, as well as Republican candidates of the past, Bob Dole and most definitely, gentleman John McCain.

"The Republican Wimp Factor is something that has dominated the party since FDR was president.

"This led to losing days of me-tooism, which made the Republicans a predictable minority party for over 40 years.

"Richard Nixon broke the mold as a vice-president, but by 1971 he was a Keynesian. Barry Goldwater and Ronald Reagan were the only Republicans with a radar pulse since Teddy Roosevelt.

"They both had passion and the desire to return to the simpler days of the Republic"

Republicans have not only become wimpy on conservative issues, fiscal, social, and moral; they are also stupid, looking to Democrats for their next move. The bottom line on why it is time for conservatives to get it going ourselves comes from Douglas MacKinnon in late spring 2013. His article for Townhall.com is very compelling. Too bad it is so true.

"If you are a conservative and someone who believes in the foundation of traditional values, then it's time to face a sad truth -- the Republican Party of 2013 and still in 2016 is all but useless to you.

Be it the current and exponentially growing scandals of Benghazi, the IRS deliberately targeting conservative groups, or the Obama administration trying to intimidate -- and potentially jail -- certain members of the media, or the immigration "debate," one thing is all but certain: The

Republican "leadership" and its lieutenants will eventually roll over and look the other way."

Until Trump came along and these leaders quickly joined the "Never Trumpers." most Americans did not know that elitist establishment Republicans were against the people—even conservative people. Now, these same wimps are joining the Democratic Party and singing loud: "Heil Hillary!"

And, so I am using this forum to add my voice to the long chorus of conservatives who are fed up being victimized by the Republican Party. We need to have the courage to change the elitist candidate and the Party itself if Republican leadership will not. We already got our candidate, Trump. When he is elected, we can work on changing the Party and changing its name.

When I first conceived of the notion of this book, I was hoping that I could get a great conservative spokesperson, such as Rush Limbaugh or Michelle Malkin, or Laura Ingraham to co-author it. I thought of Mark Steyn and Mark Levyn also but my attempts to contact any of these stalwart conservatives were futile.

I suspect they all have their hotlines so they can communicate among each other but, no matter what I tried, I could not get a nibble. Now, I regret to say that Mark Levyn is for Hillary. Note to Sean Hannity: Levin is not so great after-all. Or maybe he just is not smart.

So, here I am again, a voice crying out in the desert, hoping to be heard by conservatives so that together we can change the end of America from something that must be to something that might be. The Republicans are playing the part of Scrooge, but Dickens may very well have written a few different endings. My advice to conservatives is that we can no longer count on Republicans to fight our battles for the values which we hold dear. Donald Trump has no problem handling most of our load.

I am especially pleased, however, that my local paper published a short letter to the editor that I submitted to their mailbag a few months ago back in 2013. In it as you will see, I publicly asked some of these same prominent conservatives for their help with this book. I did not really expect that they would hear about this piece in the Times Leader from Wilkes-Barre PA, but "Hope springs eternal."

This is the article I wrote that was published by the Times Leader in Wilkes-Barre PA on Sunday August 4, 2013.

Replace the GOP with Americans

"I am working on a new book that I plan to title, Kill the Republican Party. (Subsequently there was an alternate renaming to Bring on the American Party, [which did not stick] I would love to get a great spokesman of conservatism such as Rush Limbaugh or Michelle Malkin, to co-author it but so far they are too busy with their shows and premium subscribers to respond to my many inquiries. Maybe eventually, they will hear my entreaties and help the American cause. [Call in when you have a chance and ask them to add to the follow-up, or perhaps a reprint.]

The book will be about how the Republicans have chosen to abandon conservative Americans so they can become the ME-TOO Democrat Party and possibly trick some otherwise fine conservatives into thinking that conservatives have a bad message for the country. We don't!

Unfortunately, Republicans do not believe they need conservatives any more in their Party. They know we do not agree with them while they choose to lean towards the same progressive agenda as our most un-trusted liberal friends. Yet they think we do not matter. We matter more than anybody thinks!

Don't you think that we Libertarians and Republican conservatives and even folks like me, who are bona fide conservative Democrats should be able to join together to form something to replace the anachronistic Republican Party.

It should be the American Party since the Republicans and the Democrats have chosen to unite to become fully self-serving in their treatment of the American public. Neither the Democrats nor the Republicans in Congress care about regular Americans… Democrat and Republican lawmakers are simply corrupt. They both choose to trick Americans into thinking they are on our side. They are not on our side…

Democrats of yesterday (not their leadership) are now conservatives. Today's takers from the treasury are now Democrats. Today's conservatives that think they are Republicans are reminded every day that the real Republicans do not want conservative Americans in their ranks.

Years ago I defined a Republican as somebody with over $50 million in the bank. Maybe it is more. I think if the conservatives without $50 million in the bank left the Republican Party and formed the American Party, this would be a bullet that would decimate the Republican Party. The negative consequences of the Party's death are greatly exaggerated. Let them swallow their wealth.

The American Party can become a party to embrace real Americans. Let the Republicans and Democrats swim in their own brine of corruption.
"

Signed, Brian Kelly

Well, you can see I had to get that off my chest, I now know that regular Americans know how I stand. Don't all conservatives feel as I do? Don't you wish that elite establishment Republicans who still have conservative values could regain control of the Party from those we call RINOs? It does not seem likely, however. It appears the best solution is to bring forth *The*

American Party and conservatives must then exit the Republican Party gracefully. But, first things first! Let's get Trump elected!

Republicans have chosen to abandon conservatives

Republicans have chosen to abandon conservative Americans so they can become the ME-TOO Democrat Party. My Republican brother Joe calls his new party Democrat-Lite and he is not happy at all about the change. He was not asked about the platform going liberal progressive. I suspect that many Americans feel the same. It is very proper to call each and every one of the new Republican leaders, RINOS. I am so pleased that Rump took it to them all in the 2016 Republican Primaries. Aren't you?

Conservatives have a good message for the country but now their party, the Republicans have chosen not to carry that message on their regular channel. This new "Democrat-Lite" Party idea should fill real Republicans with enough disgust to stop the RINOS. Yet, in thirty years as I look back, it has not done the trick. My fear, as a conservative, pro-Trump Democrat is that it is not disgusting at all to the leaders of the Republican Party. If I am correct, we are all in more trouble than even most conservatives think.

Unfortunately for good conservative Americans, and those non-conservatives who may not realize they benefit from jobs and fiscal stability, the new Republican attitude does not need conservatives to make it work for them. Democrats have convinced this week brood that they should see conservatives as an embarrassment to the Republican Party.

I counter that when they express their liberal views about which we disagree whole-heartedly, we conservatives are now embarrassed that we ever had faith in such an organization. It is now in the open as conservative bloggers and Talk Show hosts are hammering Republicans for abandoning conservatives. They still talk about replacing Trump even though he won the Party's nomination. Let us cast the elitists from the Party and rename it with a more American friendly name such as The American Party.

The GOP knows that we, the conservative unwashed, living in front of the locked gates, do not agree with them. Since they continue to lean towards the same progressive agenda as our most un-trusted liberal friends, logic suggests they want conservatives out of their Party. I think it is time to go. Just say the word! Let's let President Trump lead us to a better place.

All conservatives, whether Libertarian, Constitutional, Green, Republican, or even folks like me, bona fide conservative Democrats, should not have to depend on lousy, wimpy, weak, gutless, wussy Republicans to carry our message and fight for our fights in the Congress. As we engage with other conservatives, we must replace the Republican Party with another party which for now, it seems quite proper to label *The American Party*.

After all, Republicans and Democrats have chosen to unite to become one blob of nothingness that at its root basics does not care about conservatives or Americans of any ideology. Neither party cares any longer about the American public. Regular Americans are not on the two-party agenda.

Instead, the corrupt politicians behind these parties choose to trick all Americans into thinking they (the politicians) are the blessing we have sought. It is not true! They advocate principles that would or should make us all want to throw-up. Instead of throwing up, let's do what our parents would have done. Let's throw the bums out! Let them all throw up in their exodus for having been defeated by conservative voices. Let Trump win bog-time.

When you look at the evolution of thought, it is easy to see why Democrats, such as my father, and later myself from the 1960's and 1970's are now conservatives. Most of US, who began as Independents or Democrats, have not yet made the switch to Republican because the Republican Party has not been a receptive host for real conservatives.

One thing we must all agree upon however is the fact that those Americans content enough with their lives to take from the US treasury are 99% Democrat and 1% in need of real help.

Conservatives have always wanted to make it on their own. No wonder the US is in such a sad state with the palms of so many American hands facing up, looking for alms, though they have no reason to be poor in the first place. America is not about a handout. It is about a helping hand but more than that it is about a calloused hand that does the work needed for every day to be successful.

Unfortunately, the Republican Party no longer knows how to connect with Americans though its core message is mostly sound. Most people are conservative but are lured into periods of progressivism when life does not deal a fair hand.

The bad news for America suggests that Republicans seem to be prepared to lose the next set of elections rather than admit that their base is conservative and that Trump is a good guy! Conservatism is the only hope for America as it will bring back our economy and give those starving for meaning, a meaningful and high paying job. Just look at what is happening in the Dakotas if you need proof of how well Americans can do financially in 2017.

The way I see it, Party elitists should look at how it really is. Republican leaders must stop plotting against their base and their own candidate. When people really hurt, they need temporary help. They do not need a lifetime of Obama's help with Obama in charge of their every move. Obama and the unlikelihood but possibility of a Hillary Administration unfortunately offers nothing but permanent help.

The Obama / Hillary brand of help condemns a human being to a life of sucking up to government. Republicans will pay dearly in future elections for aligning with Democrats to put forth such an asinine strategy that most real Americans are against.

Meanwhile, conservatives cannot afford to depend on such willy-nilly thought as that which pervades the Republican Party today. For people who are known as stodgy, why the ambivalence? Why not say we love or hate conservatives, and then once that is in the open say who it is that you now love. I hope it is not Hillary as she really is crooked.

Unfortunately, with no statements, the Republicans lose by default thought. In this case, the default is that Republicans now love Democrats and so, another great question is "Who needs a two-party system?"

Conservatives as all people have a survival instinct and Republicans, who once espoused conservativism at the grassroots level, are now so ambivalent that even Fox News cannot figure out what Republicans really want to do.

Conservatives have come up with an answer: "Real Republicans unfortunately and apparently do not want conservative Americans in their ranks." Thus, conservatives must find an alternative means to save America, Republicans have not been and certainly are not inclined to help.

I have been watching this game for a long time.

Being a small businessman, I have a hard time understanding what motivates the leadership of the Republican Party other than self and selfish interests and gifts from lobbyists.

The Republican Party for years has embraced conservatives such as me, though I was a Democrat by registration for most of those years. When I tried to differentiate conservative from Republican, years ago I defined a real Republican as somebody with over $50 million in the bank. Maybe it was more. Maybe it still is more. Most Republicans cannot afford to be real Republicans but regular American conservative Republicans have never been treated so small before this brand of RINO leadership got control.

Perhaps I was wrong on my numbers. Perhaps not! Regardless, those Republicans with $50 million or more in the bank are leading the Republican Party away from its conservative roots. They have forgotten what it is like to be real Americans with real needs. It seems they simply no longer care about conservatives—especially those of US who do not like the real rich business-oriented Republicans hiring illegal labor to take our jobs.

So, my thesis is that those conservatives without the requisite $50 million in the bank should leave the Republican Party and, along with those of US who are not comfortable in spelling "million"—we should form "The American Party."

I see this as the bullet that would soon deprecate the Republican Party as few members of the party have $50 million in the bank, but most are conservatives. How can any political party exist without members? If Republicans want conservatives in the GOP ever in the future, they will have to fork over a lot of their funding for conservative causes.

Some suggest that the way to win is to out-fund the opposition. Would this not be nice? But if the GOP plays the money game all the time, how can this work for conservatives? It cannot! The GOP does need those "nasty conservatives" to vote for them or they cannot have enough people to win any election. If the GOP needs help then they better figure a way to give conservatives some funding and a reason to support the parts of the GOP platform that remain conservative.

Well Too Late! All by ourselves, we conservatives found Donald Trump who happens to have his own money and he kicked sixteen other respected Republicans off the stage, some with over $100 million in funding and he is now our Presidential nominee. We are going to make him our President.

From my eyes, the negative consequences to America of the Republican Party's death are greatly exaggerated. I would suggest that along with the $50 million each, Republican elitists should be permitted to swallow and choke on the rest of their wealth. It is annoying to regular Americans that the Republican elite establishment might be intentionally harming America for its own benefit, with help from their new friends across the aisle. It really upsets me that such otherwise fine human beings (new Republicans), who can do so much for America, have signed up to be Democrats without telling US outright that we are on our own.

Shame on the leaders of the GOP!

Chapter 3   The History of Political Parties Part I

The American system today is basically two parties

As many know, in many countries around the world, there are often more than just several political parties. Yet, in the United States there are only two parties that are consistently competitive in elections.

Why is this the case? Are there any prospects of a third party emerging that can be as powerful as the Republicans of 1854? Will conservatives consider the Reform, Green, Constitutional, or Libertarian Parties? Are these parties really competitive with the Democrat and Republican Parties? In our lifetimes, have we ever seen third parties being successful in American politics? No, No, No, and No again, and that is why it is the case!

The American system is commonly called a "two-party system" because historically, there have been only two major political parties with candidates competing for offices (especially in federal elections). The first two political parties had their origins in the debate over the ratification of the Constitution--the Federalists and Anti-federalists.

Today, the Republican and Democratic Parties dominate electoral politics. Almost every federal or state-level elected official in the United States is either a Republican or a Democrat.

In fact, in the United States Congress, there are only two members in the US Senate that are not either Republican or Democrat.

They are Senator Bernie Sanders of Vermont (The Bern) and Senator Angus King of Maine. Both are Independent. Senator Joe Lieberman also held the distinction for years, while he caucused with the Democrats. Every other House member and Senator belongs to either the Democratic or Republican Party. That gives US an idea of how difficult it is to run for office without one of the two party's backing. It is virtually impossible.

The deck is stacked against true Americans who simply want to represent their neighbors and friends (constituents) to help the folks back home as well as the country as a whole. Both major parties will gang up on any effort to create a viable third party, and sometimes they attack an independent candidate if the candidate has promise.

They may even do things that are illegal if they think they can get away with it or push the notions through the courts system. So, for conservatives, it will be difficult to break away from the Republican Party but it sure appears that it will be well worth the effort. Things have become intolerable.

Our two-party system is the direct result of the way elections are structured in the United States. Representatives in the Congress and in state legislatures are elected to single-member districts where the individual with the most votes wins. Because only one party's candidate can win in each district, there is a strong incentive for political competitors to organize themselves into two competing "teams" or parties. It saves on money and it saves on effort.

By doing so, party members and their candidates maximize their chances of winning elections. In some counties where there are multi-member districts, parties that win smaller percentages of the vote can often win some legislative representation. Consequently, in such systems, there is an incentive to form smaller "third" parties.

Other features of our system of elections at the highest levels include specific campaign finance rules, an electoral college rather than a direct vote for President, as well as rules giving various candidates ballot access—even write in capabilities. Not much of the laws governing ballot access are fair to regular Americans. They do work fine, however, for entrenched politicians.

All of these contrivances are designed by politicians to solidify the two-party system and to provide a distinct advantage for the incumbents from either of both parties. Individuals choosing to buck the system are permitted by the system to join in, but it is designed to make them all fail. Those candidates not sponsored by the elitists in one of the parties are made to look like fools if they choose to confront the constabulary—those who own the election process. The founders never thought Americans would be so slippery and so petty, but alas, we are.

We have all heard the term bi-partisan which is a duping phrase for voters meaning that when Democrats and Republicans get together to fix things, it is OK. It means that the members of the two supposed hostile parties agree.

Members of two parties violently opposed to each other's' notions have chosen to agree on certain matters that are important to citizens. Can you believe that they can do that if the fix is not in? When the parties apparently agree, and the "fix is in," it often means that somebody has been paid off, and Americans, so wanting our elected representatives to be honest give them the benefit of the doubt. Americans are inclined to give second chances and so history shows we have a problem throwing the bums out of office. Make no bones about it—all of this it is our fault and it will remain corrupt until we choose to say, "Enough!"

I tried to get elected once to each chamber of Congress. I know that it is an unfair process and that is why we get the candidates we get and that is why wimps get elected to important offices. It is almost impossible for a regular American to get elected to national office unless they are either rich, or they take somebody else's money—I mean a lot of money.

This tacit collaboration of the parties would be called collusion and it would be a crime if two businesses chose to operate that way. Can you imagine Walmart and Sears deciding to use bipartisan logic to fix the prices of similar products, which they sell?

With two parties, the one big advantage is that there can be two distinct points of view, but today with RINO Republicans opting for the Democratic Way, the two-party system is hurting America. I took no money and I got 17% of the vote in the primary for Congress in PA in 2010, while my competitors each had over $250,000 in their campaign treasuries.

Unfortunately, when our representatives spend so much time together in Washington, it is easy for them to join in unholy alliances of bipartisanship against the American people. These times in America are such times. The damage they do is worse than if Sears and Walmart got together to set prices. Yet there is no law that prohibits both political parties from thinking the same way.

If Sears and Walmart thought the same way, they would be arrested. Collusion or bipartisanship should be looked upon negatively by the people. But, first of course, the people have to begin to realize we are being snookered by corrupt politicians, and we have to be willing to push back against this corruption, or we must be willing to see America collapse in front of our eyes. In many ways, Donald Trump's rise is a direct reflection of Americans being mad as hell about the collusion of representatives for their own selfish interests.

Having run both for Congress and for the US Senate, I can give testimony that the deck is stacked against anybody without the support of one of the major parties. In other words, those features of our US election system that brought forth the two-party system also serve to effectively block the emergence of third parties or solo efforts by citizens, such as you or me, to seek office.

If you love America as I do, try it yourself some time if you doubt me. Good candidates without political experience are excluded from the process. Ironically, most people before the Trump days would see a non-politico such as I running and they would explain him or her away as not having experience. If you think about it, experience is an enabler of corruption and so Americans should look for fresh blood, not political hacks.

Of course there are third parties such as the Libertarian Party, the Green Party, the Constitution Party, and others. Unfortunately, these parties have had little impact on the political process because their concerns have been fragmented among multiple constituencies.

There have been a number of other political parties that have come and gone over the years. History shows that when third parties emerge and hope to be recognized, their successes are short-lived. In most cases, the American public is convinced that they would be throwing their votes away if they chose to vote third party v. one or the other two major parties.

Though this is true in particular elections, the fact that strong third parties or fourth parties have not emerged is because of this popular notion. It is a self-fulfilling prophecy, which we regular people must work to destroy or only crafty politicians will be running for office.

Democrats and Republicans own the landscape and without force of some kind, they are not about to tell the American people that it is a good idea to vote third party. With no unique issues to stand on and then with eventual depleted voter support, third parties generally fade away. But, they do not have to do so, if the people can become energized.

The largest third party since the 1980s is the Libertarian Party, yet even this reasonably popular ideology with a party to match has not had much success in national elections. In the last eighty years, the left and right sides of the political spectrum have been served by the Democrats on the left and the Republicans on the right. Ironically the US political parties are not shaped as the corresponding parties in other parts of the world.

For example, economic liberalism and classical liberalism have a central principle of limited government. Not so in the USA! These notions are supported by conservatives, who traditionally have been allied to the Republican Party in the US, and not to the left-leaning Democratic Party.

As a conservative Democrat, I have never had a deep love for the Republican Party. Yet, being conservative, I have always respected the Republican platform as an alternative to the liberal progressive agenda of the Democrats.

Republicans offered the only conservative game in town that could win a national election. Consequently, rather than vote for progressive liberals, or choosing to dilute my vote by going Libertarian, I found myself often voting Republican. A notable exception to this was when I twice supported Robert P. Casey Sr., a respected Pennsylvanian for Governor of Pennsylvania.

I would not support his son Robert P. Casey Jr. if dog catcher ever became a political office in our state. I ran against Senator Casey as a write-in Democrat in the PA Senatorial Primary in 2012. Like most Republicans, Robert P. Casey Jr., a Democrat, is known as a "wimp" in his home town of Scranton PA. This particular apple fell far from the family tree, but Democrats do not care. He loves Obama and so Casey got elected twice.

Things have changed in 2016. Like chameleons, many former conservative Republicans, such as RINOs John McCain, and

Lindsey Graham, now openly embrace the principles of socialism and liberalism as espoused by the Democratic Party. Good for them. In America we are free to be who we wish. My advice on this issue is just don't ever trust them again.

Such faux conservatives, most often called RINOS by real conservatives, have taken control of the Republican Party. Conservatism in general is something Republicans are prepared to abandon. They think they have a better shot at the Hispanic vote. Therefore, more and more conservatives are looking for an effective alternative, rather than wasting votes on RINOS. Many are considering the formerly unthinkable. Should we look for a new Party to join? When that decision is made, look for *The American Party.*

I would consider joining a new Party with the right ideals. The new Party should be mostly conservative in nature and a perfect name as noted previously would be The American Party. What American would not want to be a member of the American Party if they knew it was for America and Americans?

George Washington Was Not a Two-Party Politician

Students of history know that George Washington became President in 1789, after the Constitution was ratified. He served two four-year terms while being a member of no political party. There were no real political parties in Washington's time but that did not mean that all people were in accord on matters that were political in nature.

For example, in Washington's time, there were some issues with John Adams, his Vice President and the second President of the United States. Adams had many disagreements with Thomas Jefferson, Washington's Secretary of State. Adams was a federalist (state's rights) as was Jefferson but they disagreed on many other substantive issues. At the time Alexander Hamilton, a deep American patriot and the author of many of the Federalist Papers, was Secretary of the Treasury.

Additionally, according to the Constitution, candidates for President and Vice President did not run by party affiliation but instead they ran individually. Whichever candidate received the most votes became president and whichever got the second most was elected vice president. When John Adams ran for president upon the expiration of Washington's second term, his identified favored man for the VP job was Thomas Pinckney, but he came in third. In the third election for President of the US—the election of 1796, Thomas Jefferson, not Pinckney, came in second by only three votes to Adams.

And, so, even without a political party to assure accord at the top of the government, they served together for four years. This was the only time in America's history that political opponents served in the top two executive chairs. It did not mean they had to like each other or always agree.

The election of 1796 was the last time that such a contested American presidential election would occur but this time the President and Vice President were elected from opposing tickets.

The two-party system was brewing but the laws gave it no standing. Adams' man did not automatically become Vice President. Instead and it bears repeating, Thomas Jefferson, from the opposing party was the VP in Adams first term. When the Twelfth Amendment to the US Constitution was ratified, such a result became highly unlikely in the future.

As a review, federalism is a political concept in which a group of members are bound together by covenant with a governing representative head. The term "federalism" is also used to describe a system of government such as that used in the United States in which sovereignty is constitutionally divided between a central governing authority (the federal government) and constituent political units (such as states or provinces).

Those who felt as Jefferson believed that states possessed all the rights other than those rights which they freely might choose to give to the federal government, were known as the Jeffersonians. For comic relief, please note they were not known as the "Jefferson's."

They also believed in the full authority of the body of laws known as the Constitution. Just as conservatives today, the followers of Jefferson believed that a powerful central government posed a big threat to individual liberties. Their view was that the US was a confederation of sovereign entities (the states) which chose to band together for their common good, without giving the central group power over the parts. In essence the common thought was that the states "owned" the Federal Government, and not vice versa.

Alexander Hamilton, another great patriot, who is known to have written many of the Federalist Papers leading up to the ratification of the Constitution, had a contrary opinion. He argued that a strong central government was a very good thing and in fact it was essential to the unity of the new nation. The Hamilton contingent favored a broad interpretation of the

Constitution. They saw the document as something that should and would evolve with the country as it grew.

I took time several years ago to break up the huge multi-page sentences of the Federalist Papers and I produced a book with Lets Go Publish! titled: The Federalist Papers by Hamilton, Jay, & Madison. I also wrote a small companion book to put the papers in perspective. It is titled The Federalist papers Companion. Of course I would recommend both. They sell well on Amazon and Kindle and are also available at BookHawkers.com.

Political parties were not something that the founders as well as other leading political figures of the new country, including George Washington, were concerned about. They were happy without them. They believed that having political parties, such as the Whigs, and the Tories as they existed in England, would polarize citizens and paralyze government. Look at the Democrats and the Republicans today to see why they had such great concerns. When the parties as today, go along to get along, the American people are the ones who feel the pain of their compromises.

Look what has happened to the Republicans and Democrats today. Hamilton and Jefferson both agreed with this notion. However, by the mid 1790's the two groups that they represented became separated by other ideologies and they had broken apart into separate factions. Hamilton's group became known as the "Federalists," while Jefferson's faction became the "Democratic Republicans." It is easier to refer to them as the "Jeffersonians."

The Jeffersonians differed strongly with the Hamiltonians on economic matters. The Democratic-Republicans believed in protecting the interests of the little guys -- working classes such as merchants, farmers, and laborers. They felt that an agrarian economy would best serve the regular citizens as opposed to the elites. There were no iPads or Smart Phones back then.

They did not like the idea of the establishment of a national bank of the United States (Hamilton strongly favored its establishment). They felt that such a mechanism, as our Federal Reserve Bank could be a means of usurping power that belonged to individual states. They were also concerned that such a bank would be tied too closely to the rich, and then again, the national government. They feared that people in a central government would become too powerful.

Of course, Jefferson was right, but a compromise with Hamilton would have perhaps kept the ideologues from clashing over the subsequent years. .

The Federalists saw industry and manufacturing as the best means of domestic growth and economic self-sufficiency. They favored the existence of protective tariffs on imports (Congress adopted these in 1789), both as a means of protecting domestic production and as a source of revenue. This is still a good idea and last year I wrote two books, RRR, and Saving America, both of which recommend a return to these forms of mercantilism that originally made our country strong.

Our two-party systems do not have to be!

It is probably obvious in this chapter that the two-party system is not required by the Constitution. As noted above, a number of patriots were in fact openly hostile to the idea of political parties. George Washington was one of them and he of course is quoted as being worried about the "baneful effects of the spirit of party" on the young Republic. Jefferson was even blunter in his criticism: "If I could not go to heaven but with a party, I would not go there at all."

Originally as discussed in this chapter, Hamilton and Adams won out over Jefferson but Jefferson would have his day. Ironically, Hamilton had a hard time getting his ideas across and adopted without having like-minded men on his side. So, to win passage of his programs, he formed coalitions with men of like minds and together these allies as noted became known as the Federalists. They recruited candidates to be successful in subsequent elections so as to increase their majority in the Congress.

Not to be outdone by others who did not want a reenactment of the English style Whigs and Tories on the American landscape, Madison and Jefferson, who were opponents of Hamilton's policies, formed their own political party as noted in this chapter.

The Federalists as they existed back then, were in many ways like the Democrat Party of today in that they believed in a strong central government, whereas the new Jeffersonian Democratic-Republicans believed that the federal government lacked the constitutional authority to implement Hamilton's agenda.

In many ways, they were like the strong-hearted Republicans of about ten or twenty or thirty years ago. They were very much like the conservatives of today. Because the Republicans are no longer who they once were, as I suspect you already know, I have been compelled to write this book. Would I not enjoy counsel from the great ones – Jefferson, Washington, Hamilton, and Madison? Can you imagine their perspective?

Ironically, the Democrats, as they would eventually become known, supported an agrarian-based economy that promoted the well-being of farmers and tradesmen. They were for successful industry but not for large businesses dominating the culture or large government taking what it wants in taxes.

They sure do not sound like today's liberal progressive Democrats and this explains why our parents (I am a Democrat) had no problem being Democrats. At one time, they were the true party of the people. Today, Democrats are the party of the socialist / progressives and the communists, and any citizen operating in a fringe areas. Democrats do not try to get the white vote. They love constituents who are happy with destroying America. Though I have yet to leave the Party, I sure would like to be able to help Democratic leadership move across to a different path.

The Democratic-Republicans were successful shortly after they were formed. In the election of 1800, they scored their first victory. Jefferson defeated John Adams in Adams' second attempt at the highest office in the land.

Encouraged by its success, the Democratic-Republican Party began organizing at the state and local level as well. Within just a few years, the D-R Party had become the dominant political party in the US. The egghead, Brainiac Federalists did not connect with the electorate and they appeared to represent only the elite and the wealthy portions of the American people, though this was not a fully accurate description.

Clearly there were far more people than successful people and so what Democratic Republicans could not achieve economically, they were able to achieve at the ballot box. In 1816, the Federalists were finished as they fielded their last presidential candidate, who lost in a landslide to James Monroe.

Tid bits of the two-party system on the way to today

In a two party system, just like in a basketball game, certain parties go on a run and win election after election, while the opposition party keeps losing. For example, let's jump ahead to the time between 1932 and 1980. The Democrats won seven of 11 presidential contests, and held both chambers of Congress for all but a few years. Yes, that means that the Republicans lost 4 of 11.

Backing up, as noted, the fledgling US got to test its constitutional precepts on elections way back in the elections of the late 1700's. The third one was really historic. It was one of the first peaceful transfers of power between opposing political parties ever in the political history of the world. It was certainly a first in a democracy (democratic republic).

The victorious Democratic-Republican Party were perhaps as surprised as anybody that power transferred without a fight. As an aside, as we have been promulgating so far in this book, the Democratic-Republican Party was a direct predecessor of the modern Democratic Party, and thus it is considered to be the oldest continuous political party in the world.

The notion of national conventions was not far off once the US political parties started to blossom into their current shape. The conventions were intended to galvanize party members for the coming election. The Democrats held the first-ever national convention in 1832. It was convened in Baltimore, Maryland, more or less as a big pep rally.

However, since there were always factions within parties, its upbeat tempo did help smooth over differences between several Party factions, and the principals and the delegates were able to rally the Party behind a single candidate for president.

The purpose of the convention was to choose a running mate for incumbent President Andrew Jackson. Secretary of State Martin

Van Buren was nominated for Vice President and the convention endorsed Jackson's reelection. The first US convention of all time accomplished its mission.

Before the Republican Party came into being, a phenomenon in the 1840s and 1850s, the *Know-Nothing Party,* which many called The American Party, competed with the Republicans to replace the Whig Party as the Democrats' major opposition. Sergeant Schultz of Hogan's Heroes was not the founder of the "Know Nothings." As we all know, the infamous Schultz is well known for saying: "I know nothing!"

The Know-Nothings got their name because their membership was sworn to secrecy. They were permitted to say nothing but: I know nothing about it, when asked of their party affiliation. At one point, the Know-Nothings included in their ranks six governors, five senators, and 43 House members.

Chapter 4

The History of Political Parties Part II

Who's Who—Early Politics—Democrats & the Whigs!

With the demise of the Federalists, who at the time were emulating today's Democrats in their desire for a strong central government, while they also favored the rich and the elites, the newly empowered Democratic-Republicans began to dominate the political landscape. Life was so good or so it seemed at the time that President Monroe's term of office became known as the "era of good feeling."

Ironically, things were so good that the people stopped paying attention and eligible voter turnout dropped dramatically—from more than 40 percent in 1812 to less than 10 percent in 1820. Voters felt they had little reason to go to the polls since the Democratic-Republican Party had brought them Nirvana even before Kurt Cobain.

No group of people can get along forever without a common enemy. With the Federalists out of the way, the Democratic-Republican Party began to squabble among themselves, much like the Republicans of today, who can't figure out left from right. Eventually, factions formed within the Party. They were as devastating to the health of the Party as if the Party had split in two.

To reflect the divisiveness within the Democratic-Republican Party, in the presidential election of 1824 the Party had five candidates ready to succeed James Monroe. War hero Andrew Jackson (War of 1812) won the popular vote. However, due to the Electoral College and the notion of delegates v. the popular vote, Jackson failed to receive a majority of electors.

Thus, to settle the squabble, the election was to be decided by the House of Representatives. In this interesting test of Democracy and the Constitution in action, runner-up John Quincy Adams, the son of the second President, become the victor by forging a deal with third-place finisher Henry Clay.

Jackson's supporters understandably were upset by what they saw as backroom deal-making, and splintered off to form what they called the "Democratic Party." They revived an old Jeffersonian coalition of farmers and tradesmen, and began to effectively organize at the national, state, and local level. They formed clubs and committees, holding rallies, established a chain of newspapers, and they raised a lot of money for their candidates. This technique can be used again as the secret to a successful American Party organization. We can learn lots from the past.

The rallying cry of the new Democratic Party was the elimination of corruption in Washington. Wouldn't that be nice! The more things change the more they stay the same. Think of what the Republicans would be able to do if their backers chose to control the media by purchasing news outlets. But, unfortunately for America, Republicans in 2016 have chosen to continue to be the "Wimp Party," and the elites with the money seem content that Democrats dominate the media and the elections.

Supporters of President John Quincy Adams, however, did not stand still. They responded by collecting together the rest of the factions of the Democratic-Republican Party and they joined with the outraged remnants of the old Federalist Party. They picked a poor name (Whigs) but their idea is as sound today as would be the American Party when we are ready to pull it off.

Unfortunately just as today, the Whigs, as they became known, lacked the Democrats' organization, and they were soundly defeated in 1828, 1832, and 1836. They scored their only presidential victories in 1840 and 1848 with war heroes William Henry Harrison and Zachary Taylor, respectively. It had little to do with the party message and lots to do with their outstanding candidates. The Whig Party was doomed by its own ineptness— the same kind of ineptness that is already dooming the Republican Party.

In many ways, the new Parties held the same ideologies as their forerunners. Those on opposite camps did not trust each other a bit. However, they were quite consistent in their economic policy.

The new Whigs supported a national bank and tariffs as did the old Federalists. They hoped to protect manufacturers and use industry to keep the country strong. The Democrats were against the central bank and they were for low tariffs since this helped the farmers sell their wares abroad—even though they caused non-agrarian US employees to work for companies that were hurt by lower priced imported products.

Both parties were badly split over the slavery issue. Consequently, since they did not want it to be a debate point, the parties colluded to suppress slavery from becoming a national issue, as many in the R and D parties do today regarding abortion. Despite not wanting to talk about slavery, just as abortion today, it proved impossible as feelings and emotions intensified.

The Modern Democrats and the Modern Republicans

Where there is opposition, there is opportunity. The Whigs were not much more than the old Federalist Party and their reluctance to discuss slavery became a big issue. Just as I am encouraging conservatives today to form and then join the American Party as the natural way to diminish the Republican Party that chooses to ostracize conservatives, a group of elitists liken to the Whigs; that is exactly what happened in 1854. It can happen again in 2016 and in 2020.

In 1854, a group of anti-slavery forces organized to form a third party. Out of the political party archives, they dug up the other half of the old name "Democratic-Republicans," and they took the other half as their moniker. They became the "Republicans."

There was no trace of a biased or corrupt media back then as there is today. Consequently, the regular people were not induced to hate Republicans simply because they were Republicans. Instead, the Republicans quickly attracted anti-slavery members from both of the two major parties. They also absorbed the pro-business elements of the dying Whig coalition. This is the same approach that can make the American Party an overnight success.

The first Republican candidate for president

The first presidential candidate of the new Republicans was a man named John Fremont. He is not well known in history, and was not exceedingly popular in his day. Fremont was soundly defeated in 1856.

After regrouping, the Republican Party put forth its second candidate for President, a humble man named Abraham Lincoln. Lincoln was victorious in the election of 1860 and the world changed forever. It will change again when conservatives in both the Democratic and the Republican parties of today, along with conservative Libertarians, Constitutionals, Greens, Reforms, and other parties choose to join together to form the American Party.

The success of the Republican Party with Abraham Lincoln was monumental. Most minorities, blacks and even Hispanics, think the Democrats ended slavery, but it was the Republicans. Abraham Lincoln was their man. The Republican Party became the first and only third party in American history to ascend to major party status. I am counting on the American Party to be the next!

Today, the lying progressives and liberals in the Democratic Party have used propaganda to convince the American youth and the voters who do not pay attention that the very name "Republican Party" is reason enough to vote Democrat. This theme is a theme representing the extent of the corruption of the media.

The young in America today, often called the millennials, have voted in an idealist movement that is bent on destroying all opportunity for young Americans. It is ironic that the millennials have voted for diminished personal opportunities, while receiving nothing at all in return. They have no compunction to vote for candidates that favor young Americans receiving high paying jobs or for a Party that wants America to succeed. They literally are reaping the bad crop from the seed they elected.

And so, along with many low information Americans, the "independently minded" millennials vote Democrat consistently and mindlessly, because their professors tell them to do so. This of course places them and their to-be progeny on the road to big time failure.

Meanwhile, their liberal progressive parents, with whom they are forced to live since they cannot find meaningful work or any work at all, cannot understand the cause and effect nature of life. So much can change at the ballot box but the idealists refuse to see it, and they continue to vote with their heart instead of their head, and their children continue to suffer.

It would be nice if Obama, Hillary, and the Democrats had a plan to make the economy of the US vibrant again. They do not and it is intentional. They prefer that millennials and others continue to have deep gratitude to big government for giving them food stamps and cell phones and other goodies, rather than giving them positive prospects for a good life, and a real opportunity to achieve it. Donald Trump will change that for the better.

Ironically, the youth borrow money from Obama to go to school and when they graduate, they cannot get a job. Their far left professors blame George Bush yet no employer cares about how much the graduates hate the former President. If they want government handouts, they won't get jobs. Additionally, the new capitalistic Obama-run Student Loan Company finds nothing wrong with banking $fifty billion of student loan profits just last year alone, which of course, today's millennials must pay back.

Yes, our government is profiting on the losses of our student children and yet nobody is howling with complaints because it somehow helps Obama and his ideology. "Don't do anything to hurt Obama," is the cry across liberal America whiles all liberal Americans and all other Americans suffer the pain of his incompetence. The same for Hillary. Even if she lies, the progressive press does not want anybody to do anything that hurts her chances for the presidency. What happened to telling the truth?

Where are Republicans on this travesty? Why have the Republicans not explained the cause and effect to theoretically bright college graduates, rather than just sit down and take it? Republicans are MIA on just about everything that can help defeat Democrats and on what is right for the USA. They are too busy protecting themselves from a Donald Trump presidency because he will make America fair again and the elite establishment will no longer be the party bosses.

Let me go over this again in case a millennial is reading this section. It seems that millennials love Obama because he is charismatic and he is a supposedly the exclusive proponent of all good things. He gives them food stamps and cell phones though they know they do not deserve them and so they thank him even though they had to move in with their parents and they no longer have any possibility for a job in the Obama-run economy. Sounds like there is a logic disconnect someplace in that scenario.

This group of young Americans has no hope and will have no hope until they smarten up and stop following the Pied Piper. They know they have no hope because the part of industry that can give them high paying jobs has been maligned by Obama and the corrupt media and it has fewer and fewer jobs to offer Americans, while it is fighting for its economic survival. Meanwhile the President asks Americans to permit illegal and legal aliens to take the jobs that Americans otherwise would be able to claim.

The media thinks it is better for a Guatemalan or Chinese student to get the better college-level graduate jobs in America. Ironically, today's youth has voted for the man who keeps creating their pain. Yet, because they choose to be blind, they still blame Republicans. Some continue to rant that George Bush did it! And Republicans are so smart, they stand silent and choose not to defend themselves while the blamers are unemployed.

It is time for another Kingston Trio favorite in which one of the verses is "When will they ever learn?" Maybe never! Ideologues fall hard! Where have all the flowers gone?

When will they ever learn? When will the Republicans ever learn because they choose to act defenseless in the middle of an all-sides assault by progressive liberals and their buddies—the well-duped millennials in the Democratic Party. He, who chooses not to defend himself, loses. It is that simple. Conservatives are sick of losing and so the American Party offers great hope.

What happened to Republicans after Lincoln?

We all seem to know the history of the two major political parties after the Civil War. From the time of the War, Republicans dominated national politics from 1860 to 1932, controlling Congress for most of that time. They won all but four presidential elections. During this period, the Republicans stood for making America strong.

They espoused policies good for America. They brought forth national expansion, laissez-faire (free market) capitalism, and without the sanity that the Republicans brought to the American business climate, Americans today would be speaking German, Russian, or Chinese, and perhaps all three just to buy a bar of soap.

The Democrats were the party of immigrants, farmers, and tradesmen, or so it seemed. Yet, many Democrats worked in the factories, including the auto workers, and they made as much money as many white collared Republicans. How soon we forget what good industry brings to a country.

The Republicans have forgotten their message, and that is why nobody knows how good they can be. Today, Republican Wimps in the leadership roles in the Party do not permit conservatives or the rest of their membership to climb out from under their school-desks. If they do not hear the conservative voices pushing them to man-up, then it is the right time to bring on the American Party. Most of the Republican base and a substantial portion of the Democratic base are poised to become the American Party.

Chapter 5   The History of Political Parties Part III

The Wilson Years

On the way to FDR, there was nobody besides Woodrow Wilson who did more for socialism than any other president. Wilson fully enabled a revenue source that kept on giving for the Wilsonian notion of redistribution of wealth. Wilson never asked, "Where's the beef?" He knew that it existed in the Personal and Corporate Income Taxes that he made happen while he was president. Wilson was the guy that got to distribute it all.

Just like I am continuing to suffer from January 2009 to January, 2016, I cannot think of something more desired by conservatives in his time than Woodrow Wilson's term having expired. Americans had to put up with Wilson from March 4, 1913 – March 4, 1921. I suspect a few good Americans, not necessarily the elites, dropped full kegs of tapped American beer on the streets when Wilson's financial reign of terror on the working class ended.

The Personal Income Tax brought in under the Wilson regime was the source of funding that took the earnings of hard working Americans and gave them to those who had not earned the wages. This was once known as "relief" but now is known as redistribution of income. Americans have always been chumps for sob stories and Wilson was full of them and other things that hurt the sustenance of the country.

Wilson's adoption of the Personal Income Tax gave all presidents from that point on in history, including Barack H. Obama the opportunity to use the public's money for social engineering endeavors. All such schemes are against the Constitution but this did not matter to Wilson, FDR, LBJ, or Obama. With lots of revenue from the new taxes, Wilson was able to achieve his goal of using "practical means of realizing for society the principles of socialism" by unshackling state power.

Wilson had a radical political agenda but was unable to achieve all of his socialist objectives in two terms--but he tried. He caused a lot of lasting damage nonetheless. His revitalized democratic political science notions addressed the issues he identified. Wilson had a "different" view of policy, organization, and administration and he brought this view to his actions through his long career in the academy and in politics, and as president.

Having eradicated the significance of individual rights for democracy in his writings, Wilson went on to decree that the Constitution was not the final word. He was not a fan of the Constitution and he strongly advocated eliminating the separation of powers. From his perspective, just like Roosevelt and Obama ruling by Executive Orders, Wilson hoped it would unleash unlimited majority party government for his Party. Wilson, though a Democrat believed he could bring practicality to the demands of socialism, and he openly suggested that socialism should be the ruling ideology of his Party.

Thankfully, America is structured to survive people like Woodrow Wilson, Lyndon Baines Johnson, Franklin D. Roosevelt, and Barack H. Obama, and their innate desire to crush America, the land of the free. Wilson would have done well as President of the USSR. Over time, poor leaders such as Wilson and Barack Hussein Obama are apt to appear, hoping to take all Americans down a trail that the founders never imagined. We can avoid another tyrant by saying no to Hillary Clinton

The Roosevelt Years

One can make a great argument that the two party system has not served America so well, yet even those founders that wanted no parties recognized that a "no party" system simply could not work for politicians. The current system therefore is rigged for politicians by politicians and ballot access is denied regular citizens by elite lawmakers from both of the main parties.

If great minds from many political parties were permitted into the power structure during the Great Depression, and if their ideas were truly evaluated, Roosevelt could not have postponed the recovery as he did, until his death.

Few of US can name even a few things that politicians do well, other than breathe, consume resources, and spend other people's money. Try running for any elected office, and you will quickly see that the political classes, who inherently are incapable of governing, are very capable of creating a thousand obstacles for any regular American to be elected to serve the public.   Look at the trouble Donald Trump is having with the traditional elitists. He will be a breath of fresh air for America.

Some call Franklin Roosevelt's victory in 1932 as a "realignment" of the political parties. The Great Depression was in full bloom, and Herbert Hoover had had a tough time making things better for Americans. Liberals would say that the Republican policies of industrialization, high tariffs, and unregulated commerce caused the depression, and when they were replaced by Roosevelt's New Deal, things got better. This unfortunately was not the case for many poor Americans, but just like in Obama times, Roosevelt did not let bad news leak out of his White House.

The New Deal was characterized by many as a patchwork of federal spending programs and government regulations designed to create a social safety net for low-income Americans, particularly union workers. Though there were breadcrumbs for new immigrants, minorities, and small-business owners, there was little cause and effect improvement. Eventually everything got better when the war economy began.

However, Roosevelt is not credited with all the major solutions during his 12 + years. He was the war President from 1939 to 1943 and then he was elected for his fourth term while the war was in full bloom in 1944. He was clearly America's commander in chief and a great hero during WWII. Few Americans did not credit Roosevelt for America and the allies winning the big war. Today, Barack Obama is happy playing footsie with our enemies. Hillary Clinton as Secretary of State did the same and will do more damage if elected president.

By the end of WWII, the USA had placed the Great Depression in the annals of past history and from its war manufacturing prowess, the country became one of the most powerful nations in the world. Nobody could compete with America. Of course Harry Truman was President at the war's end. FDR passed away on April 12, 1945, about five months before Truman ended the war. .

The Commander in Chief for most of WWII, FDR, was almost perfect in the war as he used all of his domestic talents, including fireside chats to lead the war effort. He was inspirational. He enlisted the support of the American people to help win the war. He was a great cheerleader but with sincerity.

If he had another motive in his Fireside speeches other than what was best for America, it was undetectable by normal people as well as a discerning press. He was simply a hero in this regard and most Americans either never blamed him or forgave him for his poor economic policies. After the War, the economy boomed.

Like many before him, Roosevelt's war record was not perfect. But, there are few historians that suggest that if somebody other than Franklin D. Roosevelt were president, the war would not have gone so well for the US and its allies. Yet, none of these war successes ever made FDR a great economist.

Without the war, there are a number of economists who suggest that Roosevelt, just like Obama, actually stopped the country from recovering sooner by whacking the producing class and limiting the number of jobs. If that sounds like Barack Obama's and Hillary Clinton's recipe for success, just as in the Roosevelt days, there will be no jobs coming any time soon.

Roosevelt needed the war and he needed Harry Truman to end it so that Americans could get back to work. Obama does not seem to think it is worth anybody's effort whether Americans are working or not, as long as his own political future was assured.

What Caused the Great Depression? Why did it take so long to recover?

Thinking through why we never got out of the Great Depression until the massive war buildup put everybody back to work, what could have been done differently? There are a number of theories as to what caused the major depression and what might have been done to help escape from this period of no hope, which is so similar to what we now experience.

Some suggest that there are **Keynesian economic theories** of demand that explain it clearly. Many quietly agree that it was the stock market crash that caused Americans to lose confidence in the ability of the country to recover. Keynesians however profess the same economic ideology that today guides Obama into being 100% ineffective. They argued that businesses had over invested anticipating additional business and when it did not come, they were forced to cut back.

Others who advocate **demand-driven** theories suggest things happened for a different reason. They say the whole deal was caused by under-consumption. Their view was that Americans simply stopped buying stuff.

There is a demand-side consensus that there was a large-scale loss of confidence when the stock market crashed. This led to an abrupt reduction in consumption and investment spending. It may very well have been temporary if it were not for the overreaction of the media (Oh woe is me!) and the government (Let's do anything to solve the problem even if it makes it worse.).

Regardless, once the people panicked and then deflation set in, more and more people bought into the idea that they could avoid further losses by keeping clear of the markets, and spending as little as they could from their meager resources. **Holding money** for those who had money therefore became profitable as money became worth more while prices dropped lower and lower.

As time went on, a given amount of money bought ever more goods, which caused more and more people to wait for prices to go down. Why spend unless you absolutely had to spend? At 314 pounds of flesh myself, I suspect it would have been a good time to go on a diet. Eat when prices are at their lowest would have been an effective maxim.

Of course, another group of folks called themselves the **monetarists**. They counsel that the Great Depression began as an ordinary recession. However, they assert that the government's monetary authorities made significant policy mistakes. The Federal Reserve, which Jefferson thought should never exist, and which Ron Paul even today wants the government to audit, and hopefully eliminate, caused a shrinking of the money supply which greatly exacerbated the economic situation. They believed that it caused a simple recession to descend into the Great Depression. Ironically at this time, anybody who borrowed to keep going had to pay more back in real terms.

These are not the only theories of how the Great Depression came about but when a sane person looks at how it was handled, and why it was so severe, it is almost as if Barack H. Obama, rather than Franklin D. Roosevelt was steering the big Ship America at the time.

A number of what are called **heterodox notions** that reject the explanations of the Keynesians and monetarists do still exist. Some new classical macroeconomists for example have argued that it was **various labor market policies** imposed at the start of the recession that caused the length and severity of the Great Depression.

Others still look at the money supply and how fed banking decisions led to what they call **mal-investment**. Marxists of course have their own point of view. They suggest that the Great Depression was merely a big symptom of the inherent **instability of the capitalist model**.

Chapter 6   Roosevelt, Obama, and the Wimpy Republicans

Milksops need not apply

I never thought of myself as a milksop growing up. When I was five years old, for example, I had a junk route where I picked up rags and papers from my "customers" with my wagon every Saturday morning about 9:00 AM. When I was ten years old, I would awaken every morning at 5:00 AM to deliver papers with my older brother Ed, and afterward, my brother Joe. When I was twelve years old while still delivering papers, I worked from 7:00 PM to 11:00 PM at the Wilkes-Barre Republic Club Bowling Alley as a pin boy. I was not a milksop or a wimp, though I hated getting up in the AM after a night pinning at the Club.

When I turned thirteen, I gave up my junk route and worked on a soda truck every Saturday for Eagle Bottling Works. I also worked every day in the summer delivering soda. I also cut grass in the summer in the evenings, shoveled sidewalks in the winter, made and sold trinkets such as Christmas's corsages from materials available at Huntsinger's Variety Store when I thought there was a market.

I did whatever I needed to do to make a buck in the off-season. My brother Ed and I served Mass a lot at St. Boniface Church but we never got paid for that. We still hope God is a good accountant—at least on the silent stuff.

I knew my parents did not have the money to provide for my entertainment—ever. When I was fifteen, as a junior in HS, I was able to pay for my date's dinner and buy my own clothes. I have never been a stranger to work, and I credit my success in life to my parents' helping me understand that hard work pays off.

Consequently, in my life I got a lot of good advice from my father and though I did not always take his advice, he was very smart and I always listened. My father influenced my decision on joining a political party when I was twenty-three years old. I was unmarried and I had just moved from Utica, New York to my home town in Pennsylvania.

I had been an independent voter for a few years after turning 21 years of age, which for me was the voting age. When I moved back to Pennsylvania, my dad suggested that I needed a political party so that I could vote in the primary in the Pennsylvania elections. Independents were not permitted to vote in primaries and they still are not permitted to do so in PA. His advice was sound and so I became a Democrat at 23 years of age. The Party was lots different then.

As time went on, my father and I watched the Democrat party morph from the party of the common man to the party of the special interests. We knew that we could no longer count on Democrats to do the right thing for the country.

Neither of us changed parties but we became far more selective in the elections and we more often than not went with the conservative candidates. There were not many conservatives in the Democratic Party so we were forced to vote Republican quite frequently.

My dad had a long-term affiliation with the Democrats. As time went by, he felt disillusioned by the new ideology of the party and he knew he did not really belong. We both felt that we could no longer trust the Democratic Party.

Democrats stopped being for the common man and began looking for special constituencies such as minority groups and groups that represented particular causes. Though Democrats still supported labor it was not for all labor. The Party began to exclusively support union labor and developed unholy reciprocal ties to the leaders of organized labor.

My father can no longer speak for himself but I know that he would advise me that we can no longer trust either party today— Democrats or Republicans. Just look at this Congress and our socialist / fascist President. Look hard at the wimpy Republicans. Is there anybody anywhere who would claim to represent the conservative voter? I know I see nobody!

While the Democrats moved to organized labor; organized labor became more socialistic / communistic, without ever using those words. They were not interested in turning off the very people who assured their election. Years ago the unions were not as associated with socialism. No longer!

Back then, labor leader John L. Lewis for one was known for his disdain for communists / socialists. In fact, in the 1920s he had systematically driven out communists and socialists from the miners' union. At one miners' convention, Lewis stopped the proceedings and pointed to a group of known communists sitting in the balcony, and he ordered them to leave. Lewis also supported Republican Herbert Hoover in the 1932 presidential election. The polarization of today did not exist. It was OK to have an independent thought.

When President Roosevelt took office, it was toward this end that in 1935 he made two far-reaching concessions to workers. He pushed through the National Labor Relations Act (also known as the Wagner Act), which finally made it illegal for employers to refuse to bargain with unions. And he secured passage of a Social Security program, by which the U.S.

government agreed to provide a minimal standard of living for the poorest families in society and for the elderly.

Both of these were great programs but it sure is a shame that it was the government, inept because it is run by politicians that was charged with making these programs work.

These two concessions proved to be the biggest gains workers won from the government during the Depression decade–gains which earned Roosevelt his legendary status as a friend to the working class. However, even though Roosevelt had promised employees that "we have only begun to fight," these were to be the last significant reforms he would grant to working class people.

In reality, these concessions were nothing more than a calculated move to capture the loyalty of the ascending labor movement for the Democratic Party, and the reason little was offered later is because the Democratic leaders were not and still are not for the people. They offer just as much as can get them elected.

The labor leaders were all too happy to deliver the non-thinking voters to Roosevelt. By raising the slogan, "The President wants you to join the union," at picket lines all over the U.S., the CIO leadership virtually guaranteed Roosevelt's continued popularity among workers. This, despite Roosevelt's boast, "I am the best friend the profit system ever had." Analysts look at these words and suggest Roosevelt was merely an ameliorator. What do you think? He surely intended to prevent revolts from below through reforms from above.

My father liked unions and he loved Franklin D. Roosevelt, but in reality most of us never realized just how socialist and pro-union Roosevelt had become. I'll come back to this in just a bit but first let me tell another short story about my father and his experience with regular unions.

When my dad worked for the Stegmaier Brewery in Wilkes-Barre PA, he loved the union more than the company. As a descendent of a union lover, I was well aware of how important the union was in my father's life. One of my newspaper customers, Henry Vivian, to whom I delivered a paper every morning, ran a barber shop and besides that; he was a great person.

Mr. Vivian was also a good tipper—but unfortunately; he was not in the union. He was excluded even from Roosevelt's New Deal. I could not get my hair cut by Henry Vivian. To live in my father's house, one of the requirements was that I get my hair cut in a union barber shop. That's just how it was.

Union people support union people. I know exactly why my dad loved the union above the company, but then the union stiffed him and a lot of folks that he had worked with for many years,

When Stegmaier went out of business and sold its label to Gibbons, my dad was about fifty-seven years old. He had a lot more work years left in him. Gibbons Brewery bought the Stegmaier Label but not the brewery facility. All of the Stegmaier property, including its major aging vats, were permitted to lay dormant until they were auctioned. Yet, Stegmaier and Gibbons had the same union.

Unfortunately for the Stegmaier workers such as my dad, the union decided that it was OK for the Gibbons Brewery to hire the younger men from Stegmaier and take the older men last, if at all. They did not have to abide by the seniority clause in the Stegmaier contract as they felt their obligation was with the Gibbons contract. Obviously, after paying union dues for years, the older men at Stegmaier, including my father, felt cheated and the oldest workers felt even worse when they learned that they had not make the cut.

So, in this instance, when the union made its decision to help the new company rather than the long-term employees of the old company, my dad knew and I knew that the union had taken the money (dues) for all those years and they had run. When the going got tough and there would be no more dues from the Stegmaier contingent, the union vacated the premises along with management. On to the next opportunity!

My dad told me that he still felt that unions could be great but if they chose not to help their memberships, as in this case, they were worth nothing. Ironically, when Gibbons began to brew Stegmaier in the Gibbons facility using the younger Stegmaier workers, my father continued Stegmaier as his favorite brew. He was a great man!

There are very few companies today, who are like IBM, where I worked in the 1970's and 1980's. At the time, they put the employee first. For this, they expected that the employee would to do the best for the company. Today, corporate greed is everywhere and it is seen more and more in the labor part of the equation.

Loyalty is not even a word used in the labor management equation. Greed is the only word. Corporations suffer from a lot of greed, for sure. IBM just this week announced that it was cutting off those retirees over 65 years old from health benefits long promised. In all fairness to unions, a good union would not have permitted this.

To be fair again, where unions rule the roost, there is a lot of union greed. In fact, it was union greed that forced GM to pay a higher wage than the market would sustain and as we know in 2008, the real GM went out of business and it was eventually taken over by Barack Obama's Government Motors.

Just like a kid selling Kool-Aid, the owners of businesses do not want to pay any more than the minimum and the workers they employ want enough to compensate for giving up their time, which often results in a certain level of enjoyment.

Traditionally, since they gained power in the 1890s, unions have provided this enjoyment factor for employees and this is why employees faithfully pay their union dues. It is not that they love the union leaders. Union members actually pay dues for their higher wages.

The notions of offshoring and illegal immigration have posed big problems for unions, none of which it seems the unions have been able to solve. The fact is that a worker has no employment rights at work unless he or she is part of a collective bargaining agreement. Yet union membership continues to go down perhaps because of stories like my dad's where when the chips were down, the union phone was not answered. Perhaps if union leaders appeared more human it would help. Many people look at the leadership, not the union worker, and are turned off at the apparent greed.

Among other problems as seen by regular Americans, labor union leadership seems to be doing poorly in terms of being a countervailing force for illegal immigrants taking U.S. workers' jobs. Despite these shortcomings, organized labor is still a very important political and economic force today, but its influence has waned markedly in recent years.

Manufacturing, where unions once thrived has declined substantially, and the service sector, where wages are traditionally low, has grown. Yet, unskilled blue collar jobs are not as abundant as in the early 1990's. The union message does not always take hold. Perhaps it is the large union dues that are a must to gain a dollar of benefits. Perhaps some people want to tough it out.

Unions have become very powerful in education and government under AFSCME and this is one of their major strongholds today. Overall the # of unionized workers in the US declines every year. The bottom line is that those people motivated to work, want to make it on their own and they do not want anything, including a union, to hold them back.

Republicans for the most part have always been allied with business. Yet, the GOP has not really been against workers per se. In fact, if it were not for successful companies, even union leaders know that potential workers would have no jobs. So, both Democrats and Republicans traditionally have had a stake in assuring that businesses are successful. Clearly, Republicans are in first place on this notion.

Unfortunately, during Obama's terms, Democrats have become more interested in being the party of free stuff and Republicans have been trying to figure out how to tell the people getting the free stuff that they love them too. They want to say that they love them as much as the Democrats but nobody really likes also-rans.

Conservatives do not like the new views of the Republican Party that winning elections is more important than doing what is right for the country. Unfortunately, no political party is trying to help businesses be successful in America and no political party is working to assure that the American people can ever get well-paying jobs again. But, if there were other than wimps in Congress, perhaps somebody would care and perhaps Americans could be placed on top of the legislative agenda again.

Power Meets Power

Whenever there is a void, there is an opportunity. The labor arbitrage of the late 19th century affected mostly unskilled workers. But in reality, all workers were affected. The greed of the Robber Barons of this era was so massive that they wanted to pay not one penny more than the most meager of subsistence. The people think this is a Republican notion. It may be depending on your perspective.

But, it is not something good for the Republican Party. If valid, it is a notion espoused by only the 1% wealthiest Republicans even today. Shame on them! Perhaps it is they who are chasing conservatives away. How well will they do with 1% of their former number, when election time comes and the conservatives are gone?

Republicans should know better and they should know that they are ruining their party and they are forcing conservatives to look elsewhere. I would not have been motivated to write a book entitled "Kill the Republican Party!" if there were not a need. Perhaps Americans can start a Party without that 1% that want to dominate all of our thoughts. We can do well because this is America. Yes, the bad guys today are Republicans who want to purge the party of conservatives such as you and me. Let's leave willingly and see how well they do without conservatives to add to their vote tally.

FDR, like Obama did not want to lose any election. So, he obliged and became a pro-union president in much the same way as President Obama. This did help the individual workers in the specific unions but it did not help all workers evenly, nor did it help America per se. Look how long the depression lasted. Look how long the Obama recession has lasted. Try to get a job! In some cases, as in the auto industry, for example, it ultimately led to the demise of both the unions and the companies.

As part of his pro-union agenda, FDR signed the Wagner Act, which forced employers to negotiate with unions that won collective bargaining elections. It also set up the National Labor Relations Board (NLRB) to negotiate and examine claims by workers of unfair labor practices by employers. Very few claims were settled in favor of the companies.

The United Steel Workers Union was formed in 1936 and gained administrative support and increased in numbers during the FDR years.

Unions were on the rise and they thanked Roosevelt by electing him four times. The Steel Union for example, told workers in collective bargaining elections that FDR supported unions and wanted workers to join unions and they got to love unions and FDR at the same time.

Union membership understandably increased dramatically during FDR's administration. It is no wonder why union members liked FDR and they all felt he was a great president, even if their neighbor could not put food on the table. In his day job of course, Roosevelt could not pull the country out of the depression.

FDR permitted strikes to occur as payback for union support, knowing that it would hurt industry. FDR did not use troops to break up strikes as a concession to unions. Other Presidents sent troops to keep America working. Just like today, everybody other than real businesses and their employees got a break. While the New Deal was not too successful in solving the economic problems of the depression, the Democratic Party continued to have the support of organized labor in all of its elections for the last eighty years or so.

Unlike Obama who rules America much like a dictator with a free hand, and no congressional restraints, FDR had his own countervailing force with which to deal in his own administration. Just as Obama is a socialist so also was Roosevelt. Thankfully, there was a person in his administration who said enough is enough. It would be nice for somebody in the Republican Party to stand up to socialism and bad policy as did Roosevelt's first Vice President.

We need a John Nance Garner Today

John Nance Garner was the 32nd Vice President of the US and he is credited with much of the heralded legislation that the FDR administration put forth in its first 100 days. From the inside, this account shows the parallel between Roosevelt and Obama, and it shows that as instrumental in Roosevelt's success as Garner was, just like Rahm Emanuel, David Axelrod and Joe Biden, even he could not make things better for a President gone awry.

In the second term of the Roosevelt-Garner administration, Garner was not seen as progressively productive for the Democrats. In fact, Garner developed a real conscience and began taking notice to the conservative side of things. The two stars of the Party began to disagree on fundamentals of government. Unfortunately for our modern day reenactment of FDR as BHO, we cannot reasonably expect Joseph Biden to man up and take Obama on as Garner did.

The main reason is that Biden is as committed to socialist / progressive notions as Obama himself. It would be nice if Paul Ryan or relative newcomers such as Lou Barletta in the House would become antagonists v. Obama. It is already refreshing to see Senators Mike Lee and Ted Cruz lead American conservatives properly. Too bad that Marco Rubio blew his credibility on the gang of eight tyrants.

Garner had a moose sized problem with Roosevelt's determination to escalate the New Deal's charter to centralize more power into the hands of the federal government. In other words, Garner believed the states had rights and should conduct their own affairs as the founders intended and the Constitution dictates. Like FDR, Obama has little concern for states' rights. Garner was not in favor of the expansion of big government regulations and the lofty spending programs that FDR was bringing on. In 2013, by their inaction, the Republicans appear in simpatico with Obama.

As a side issue, Garner was a stalwart in the Democratic Party and he saw the Party as a bastion for American workers. He was not interested in fundamentally changing the Party. He was

100% against FDR having the ability to change the Democratic Party in any substantive way.

Though a Democrat, Garner had a lot of conservative ideas and he was like a Jiminy Cricket in the ear of President Roosevelt. Roosevelt of course never met a liberal progressive program that he did not like. Would it not be great if Joe Biden reads about John Garner, and decides that he too can be effective for Americans? Unfortunately I do not think we will see VP Joe Biden stand up for his country any time soon.

Labor and labor unions were a cause to battle and as noted previously, perhaps they have always been. Garner who was not always known as a conservative per se or he would not have made it to the Roosevelt ticket, objected to New Deal pro labor legislation initiatives such as the Wagner-Connery Act of 1935 and the Black-Connery bill of 1937. Garner was more conservative than John Boehner and Mitch McConnell could ever hope to be. And, more importantly, he worked for America and Americans.

Garner was also against the1936 sit-down strikes because they hurt the country, and instead of being blindly ideological for his President do or die, as current Democrats choose to be, Garner took the side of business owners. Their property rights were violated by these actions. Roosevelt, on the other hand supported these tactics as it helped him maintain popularity with his socialist / progressive base.

Roosevelt had picked Garner as his VP because he was the popular and powerful Speaker of the House at the time. Like Obama, Roosevelt was a politician who knew how much Garner would help him "garner" enough votes to be elected the first time, and the second time.

After the first term, Garner, as a human being, decided it was better to work for America than to work for Roosevelt's socialist progressive agenda. Don't expect Biden or Boehner to come to that conclusion for they would then have to take on "the One."

Consequently, because he had misgivings with the FDR agenda, Garner lobbied legislators in Congress who were working to undermine the freedom of such strikes via legislation. These legislators felt it was hurting America's prospects for recovery and success.

Garner's team won the day and Garner made his stance very publicly by jumping down from his presiding VP seat to offer his congratulations. Roosevelt was perhaps not surprised; but surely he was not pleased.

Roosevelt wanted to control the Supreme Court.

In early 1937, Roosevelt revealed his intentions to steal power from the Supreme Court. His idea was to reorganize the whole court by assuring that six liberal judges would be appointed by the President hoping to have his liberal legislative agenda approved by the court if he was ever taken to task.

Garner was concerned about the problems Roosevelt was causing among Democrats. He wanted to assure Party unity and he felt the President was handling such a delicate proposal in a reckless manner.

Neither man ever completely trusted the other again. Garner eventually admitted that he was very concerned about Roosevelt as President. He saw him jeopardizing the legislative program by giving out premature information, and he was concerned that Roosevelt wanted too much power. Garner said that "He has changed in office. He does not delegate. His nature is [to] want to do everything himself." Garner was in the grave when Barack H. Obama took over the US, but he surely would have offered similar commentary about our President. .

The liberal / progressive President Roosevelt had little use for conservative Democrats in Congress. Very much like our own President Barack Obama, he wanted to be able to purge the Party in the next Congressional election and gain seats by replacing Republicans.

Roosevelt's methods were not very valiant and he irritated more Democrats than Republicans along the way. Republicans emerged as the winners of Roosevelt's tussle with his own Party. In the next election, the GOP gained eighty-one House and eight Senate seats, while only one of Roosevelt's primary election targets (Representative John J. O'Connor of New York City) lost.

There was no Internet; there were no Cable TV stations; there was no TV at all; there were no iPhones or iPads or any means of communication that we have today so many Americans were not aware daily of Roosevelt's struggles with his own Party. Of course the mainstream press were a bit honest back then and they reported in print and radio media quite well but still most Americans felt that Roosevelt, no matter what, was their hero, and continually worthy of praise and reelection.

Congress did get the message on Roosevelt, however, especially those in the Republican Party and those with conservative, Constitutional leanings. Congress said "no" to just about everything Roosevelt put forth in his third term, including an undistributed profits tax, government reorganization, increased funding for the Works Progress Administration, and a revision of the neutrality laws.

Like Wilson before him and now Obama, Roosevelt was stopped at the gates by the Constitution and a Congress that believed in it. In today's world, with Democrats in control of everything, including the nation's K-12 school system, and Republicans not offering a peep in opposition, Roosevelt may have had his way.

This lesson was not lost on Obama's handlers and he is putting out more discredited Roosevelt ideas than even Roosevelt. This time, however, the less intelligent American population is buying it 100% and that is why Obama is more dangerous than Roosevelt. That is also why conservatives are upset with Republican wimps in Congress for permitting this small man to become so large and so hurtful to America, while they choose to permit him to do so without a whimper. .

New Dealers from way back, wanting to make America 100% socialist progressive could not stand Garner's conservatism and his occasionally coarse behavior. They also did not like that he was effective in his dealings and they noticed that he too frequently dipped into the shady style of his old-fashioned, back-room horse trading when necessary.

And, so the worst liberal progressives in the Roosevelt regime tried to undercut VP Garner. They made him the convenient scapegoat in not getting Roosevelt's agenda through Congress. Some claimed that he had knifed Roosevelt in the back. Roosevelt at the time, unfortunately for the Democrats, was doing his best to hurt his own reputation.

When 1940 came, there was another election and again Roosevelt emerged for his third try as the candidate of the Democratic Party. Garner had had enough and expressed major concern that Roosevelt had decided to try for a third term. To help stop Roosevelt for going for another term, Garner told the press that at the inauguration ceremony in 1937, he and then President Roosevelt made some decisions among themselves.

Garner noted the two had taken a mutual pledge to retire at the end of that term. Roosevelt saw the pledge differently as events unfolded abroad that apparently prompted him to run for a third term. His team argued that the volatility of the international situation made his presence indispensable. In many ways the Democrats of today see Obama as indispensable; so who knows whether Hillary will ever get her chance in 2016. Most nationalists, populists, and conservatives sure hope she does not.

In 1939, Garner was so frustrated with FDR that he tried to become the first vice president of the modern era to challenge his own chief executive for the office of President. He knew he had no chance and he was ready to retire. He was so upset about Roosevelt running a third time, that he joined the "Stop Roosevelt" movement.

In 2012, a similar "Stop Obama" movement went nowhere as the President was able convince Americans that George W. Bush was still responsible for any of Obama's bad decisions. Though VP Garner, a Democrat, felt he was the only candidate with a chance of attracting enough support to convince the President to retire, the American people were caught up in Roosevelt as their hero.

The same brood of Americans would be voting for Obama for term # 5 and # 6 before he might reluctantly retire. Watch out Hillary! Conservative congressmen praised Garner to their favorite reporters. The press, in turn, was usually eager to carry "good copy" about the legendary cowboy vice president (Garner) who rode herd on Washington and plotted in the cloakrooms. But, he did not carry the day when he challenged Roosevelt.

Hitler and Roosevelt

In 1940, Hitler's regime was making moves everywhere across Western Europe. Roosevelt, who had earlier warned about Hitler, was thus precluded from any challenge to his nomination. Again, he became the candidate after just the first ballot at the Democratic National Convention in Chicago. Nobody, including Garner, had achieved as much as 100 votes in this election. Would Garner have been a better President because he was not as political as Roosevelt? Of course!

Garner it is reported, did not even vote in the 1940 election. He got out of the way and went home to Uvalde, his home in Texas. He lived there after his retirement until his death at the age of ninety-eight—twenty-seven years later. He was almost 99.

In his memoirs, Garner thought that he may not have played his cards correctly. He was very concerned that Roosevelt was undermining the founders' notion of America and the Constitution. He wished he had done his best to check Roosevelt's power grab at the gate. He felt that if he had tried more vigorously, he could have talked Roosevelt out of a lot of things. He felt that these conversations could have been his contributions to America. Is there anybody like Garner out there, who can mitigate the next three years of Obama? Wouldn't that be nice?

Roosevelt got over Garner quickly. He picked a different kind of guy than Garner in 1940 as his VP—Henry Agard Wallace. Mr. Wallace was seen as the antithesis of Garner. Wallace could not even get access to Roosevelt or his chief minions and so he could do nothing to undermine this President or help the country as Garner was able to do.

Joe Biden had a chance to learn a lot about being a better man. Garner was a parochial thinker, with his own isolationist convictions. Wallace was a nobody, who stayed a nobody. He lacked legislative experience and was not a power broker in the Party. Joe Biden chose not to look for a shot at the presidency, but it would have been nice if he were a good Vice President for America like John Garner.

Ironically, Garner was a specialist in an office that would soon require generalists. Look at VP Biden and tell us all what his specialty is or was! Garner was silent as an administrator when silence was revered. Then came the other Washington-based vice presidents just before the age of modern telecommunications and travel. These later VEEPS were wide-ranging campaigners, public spokesmen, and foreign emissaries, but as we have seen, other than Dick Cheney, they offered little value to their respective administrations.

During his first term, Garner may have made a more valuable and positive contribution to his administration than any of his predecessors, but his actions in the second term did more to undermine the administration than those of any vice president since John C. Calhoun. Chosen to balance the ticket in 1932, Garner felt obligated to use all of the formal and informal powers of his office to protect the interests of the Party's conservative wing that had, against his better judgment, moved him from Speaker to Vice President.

Garner is an American hero who was the first Democrat in recorded history to go against the Democrats even though it might hurt him as an individual. Let such courage stand noticed by all Americans. Let Americans in 2013 learn from John Garner that patriotism to America does not mean loyalty to anti-American actions by any president. Do you hear that Joe Biden? Do you hear that Reince Priebus?

Chapter 7   Democrats, Unions, and Car Companies

Unions Outslugged the Car Companies

From Henry Ford's time, well over 1000 automobile companies, mostly in the mid country states, such as Michigan, came into being, manufactured extremely attractive cars, and then went out of business. I certainly will not posit that the reason for all these companies going out of business was the influence of big or little labor but surely, it would have helped if the auto industry was not known for paying excessive wages.

The wages in the industry for years put a stranglehold on every company's ability to turn a profit. By the early 1950's, most of the really little companies, many of whom made great cars, were either gone or had merged to survive. In Chapter 8, we show a sampling of some of the companies and their fabulous vehicles, which today are prized collectibles.

In the 1950's the United Auto Workers (UAW) had subsumed most of the smaller unions that were prevalent in the first half of the century. The UAW stood strong as it continues to do today. It had organized and established collective bargaining relationships with the companies known as the "Big Three"— General Motors, Ford, and Chrysler, and also with the smaller auto producers of the era—Nash Kelvinator, Studebaker-Packard, Hudson, and Kaiser Willys.

Additionally, the UAW worked with American Motors, when it was formed by a merger of Nash-Kelvinator and Hudson in 1961. Eventually all that was left standing were the Big Three as one by one the other companies went out of business or merged and / or sold off parts of the company. An example was Kaiser Willys, shoes Jeep Division still exists within Chrysler.

Unions were not the only factor in the ruination of so many car manufacturers, but they sure helped along the way. Supporting the UAW wage demands adds about $1500 or more to the price of an automobile. Therefore, it is understandable that union demands were not very popular with the management teams of any of the great American car makers. The consumer did not know exactly what part of the car price was made up of labor, and so they were more or less out of the foray.

However, Americans all seemed to know that Detroit auto employees were paid more than any other blue collar workers in the country. Unions gave management a real tough time and it literally was a survival game for the companies. If a smaller company could not produce cars, any of the Big Three would be happy to fill in the void. Knowing that consumers were not about to wait for their wheels, the car manufacturers took the union's ability to strike very seriously.

Let's look at three modern era examples of non-Big Three companies that could not make it mostly because of union troubles. Studebaker, which made beautiful cars, had big problems with an aggressive union. For years, the union saddled the company with the highest labor costs in the industry. The Studebaker Company always seemed to cave in to union demands rather than risk being put out of business by a strike. It was blackmail at its finest at Studebaker and many others.

When AMC was having tough times and was ready to go under, militant UAW locals hung tough in negotiations and assured that AMC's contracts always were non-competitive. They never gave the company a chance to survive. Their local plant costs were burdensome and higher than those of any other plants in the industry. For all of AMC's existence, the unions pretty much got what they wanted. Then AMC could not take it anymore.

One of the saddest stories of all, however, is what the UAW did to Packard. Sixty-five years ago in June 1948, the UAW struck Packard in Detroit. They also conducted a walkout at the Bendix plant, which supplied the Packard's brake systems. Later in 1948, the guards at the UAW-organized Briggs Manufacturing plant also went on strike, shutting off Packard's access to necessary parts. Three shutdowns in one year put the company in a poor position.

In 1950, the UAW led another strike against Packard and Packard finally conceded to their demands to barely stay in business. The concession took $9 million per year off Packard's bottom line. The company was hardly surviving but the UAW got is increase. Eventually Packard could not sustain the bleed and in 1956, it shut down its Detroit facility, leaving the building abandoned to this day.

It is now known as the world's largest abandoned building thanks to a union that basically did nothing but help pack the company's bags when they left town for good. Packard got out of Dodge and never came back. The UAW lost thousands of members with its closing.

Unions have a lot to do with the demise of industry in this country and yet they are held in high regard by the Democratic Party because they have a symbiotic relationship. The propping up goes both ways as union leaders and government leaders all get their backs scratched from the same pot of money. Republicans choose to stand idly on the sidelines.

The Bailout -- No Republican Response

Meanwhile, the scourge that overly militant unions take on the country is all but unnoticed by Republicans and has been for many years. There is no union story that is as disgusting as what Obama and the Democrats did to small investors in GM and Chrysler during the bailout that began late in 2008.

Yet, the wimpy Republicans maintain silence even on this fraudulent helping hand like as if it is manifest destiny that Obama and the Democrats would dominate Republicans. Remember Hillary is pro-union but only certain unions. She would not take the endorsement of the Policeman's union because she would prefer to be softer on criminals.

In August 2016, the top officials at the biggest police union in the country expressed irritation with Hillary Clinton, saying she had snubbed them.

The leader of the National Fraternal Order of Police said that the Democrat sent a signal through her staff that she wouldn't be seeking the union's endorsement.

"It sends a powerful message. To be honest with you, I was disappointed and shocked," said Chuck Canterbury, the president of the National Fraternal Order of Police.

"You would think with law enforcement issues so much in the news that even if she had disagreements with our positions, that she would've been willing to say that."

The fringe of the Democratic Party does not like police.

Donald Trump is the law and order candidate for those interested in a safe America and he may very well get the Police Union's endorsement after the snub.

Countervailing Power

One of my favorite notions regarding negotiations and conflict resolution is countervailing power. When any entity—a corporation, a union, or a government gets too strong; it is time to cut it down to size. The people, the fourth entity should be able to rely on government to fight its battles, but in recent years, government has been siding with either the corporations or the unions against the people. Without good representation, the people have no strength.

No President and no Republican, of which I am aware, after Ronald Reagan, has taken on the Democrats for their illicit love affairs with the heads of major unions. Unions are tough cookies and when Democrats play the union game, they make Republicans look like the wimps they are. And, none of this helps the conservative cause.

It is not that unions are bad or that government is bad or that corporations are bad. Again, when any of the power entities get too powerful, the others need to close ranks and defeat them. In another ten or twenty years, the process will repeat itself as another entity grows in strength, and countervailing power will be called upon again to cut it back to its proper size.

When one entity becomes too strong or allies with another, however, it is not especially easy to restore a proper power balance. Having the Republicans choose to not fight either the unions or the Democrats today makes conservatives the unrepresented minority in the country.

In the countervailing power struggle during his terms, Ronald Reagan was the right guy on the job at the right time. His job was to be anti-union and if it did not work, he would have been out of a job after his first term. Conservatives love to heap praise on Reagan because he meant business, and even more importantly; he meant what he said, and he did what he said. He was not a liar.

We cannot forget that Ronald Reagan was one of the most anti-labor presidents in U.S. history, but he came after one of the weakest pro-labor Presidents in history, Jimmy Carter. Carter needs to thank the passage of time as his history has improved with the election of Barack H. Obama. Carter is no longer the worst President of all time. Obama has him beat by a long margin. Jimmy Carter otherwise would have continued to own that distinction during the remainder of his lifetime. Hillary Clinton if elected by mistake will break Obama's record as worst president of all time. We hope it does not come to that.

Republicans never have had much regard for unions, which invariably have opposed their elections. Republicans have championed industry until recently. Now, quite frankly it is not obvious what Republicans stand for. But, Donald Trump stands for America first.

Until Reagan, no GOP president had dared to challenge labor at its core. Reagan engaged in precious little bargaining. He waged almost continuous war against organized labor. Obama as today's countervailing power, wages continuous war against Republicans and American Industry. He is the perfect countervailing power against traditional Republican and American interests. Yet, despite having control of the House of Representatives, Republicans continue to stand down as if Obama is to be feared as a human being.

Americans are not as pro-union as once thought. Unions have not been doing well in opinion polls for a long time and their membership keeps declining. They are opposed by nearly half of all Americans. Many people do not know that nearly half of those who belonged to unions voted for Ronald Reagan in 1980 and again in 1984. Union workers are tough and they admired a tough man in the White House (Reagan) representing tough Americans. We are so far from that today it is frightening.

Many of us recall that it did not take Reagan long to begin his war on unions.

It was in the summer of his first term. The "Gipper" fired 13,000 striking air traffic controllers and he destroyed their union. They thought that Reagan was bluffing. For Republicans to be respected again, whether in fighting unions, fighting for second amendment rights, fighting against nationalized health care, or fighting against turning the country over to foreigners, somebody with strong male hormones must emerge to take the Republicans away from their wimp mentality. Of course, anticipating that this is not ever going to happen, conservatives need another good option. The American Party is a salient alternative.

Let's stop for a moment and reexamine the Democrat's role in the auto bailout, and specifically let's look at what Obama did to help his friends in the leadership chairs of the United Auto Workers (UAW). Ask yourself after this little recount of the events surrounding the auto bailout: Was Obama's support for the bailout politically motivated or was it done for the good of the country?

Considering that the greatest political gamesman since Bill Clinton now occupies the White House, what do you really think? Perhaps this story, with the facts as reported by Porter Stansberry will shed some light on the continuing travails of the auto industry at the hands of the unions.

Many know Porter Stansberry as a publisher for the financial industry. Stansberry has analyzed the auto industry of today and has made a most astute observation of the GM bailout. Stansberry notes that the Obama deal was not really a bailout of the company itself, nor was it a bailout of the shareholders, who lost everything or the bondholders who lost just about everything. It was a bailout for the unions, who had become quite chummy and very supportive of Barack Obama's election hopes.

Stansberry says that "The United Auto Workers (UAW) ended up with all the money. Whether you like Porter Stansberry or not; this particular observation is spot-on.

Some may recall that Mr. Stansberry was accused of fraud and the SEC fined him $1.5 million in the incident. He denies all wrong doing. Moreover, the fine has not stopped him from doing a lot of good work, some of which, such as the auto bailout analysis is worth our time. Stansberry is not a fan of Obama's and so I immediately developed an affinity for him.

In recent times, besides his auto analysis, he predicted that beginning in 2015, there would be "a new age of American prosperity, the likes of which we haven't seen in decades." He sees it coming from, a petroleum and natural gas boom. I can see how this can happen despite Obama not providing more public lands on which to explore.

With his Nosterdamus cap, Stansberry cautions that one major negative effect of this new prosperity would be that Barack Obama, would gain a third term as President. He does not say exactly how this will happen but it may be directly by repealing the twenty-second amendment or Obama may decide to have his wife, Michelle take the job. Either way, that thought is most disconcerting to any conservative. We'll see about that; but for now, let's examine the rest of his analysis on the unions making out like bandits on the bailout.

Ironically, the government bailed out the least worthy of all of the stakeholders in GM. GM had lost its ability to profitably make automobiles, its chief product. Why? Well it was overleveraged for sure and while teetering on bankruptcy for years, it could not invest much in its own future. However, the reason GM went under was that it could not make routine profits from manufacturing cars for well over 20 years.

The solo reason GM and a number of other car companies over the years couldn't make a profit on cars was because their labor costs had soared; were out of control; and the future labor costs looked like they would be even higher. Ironically, at $56 per hour- over $116,000 per year per employee, GM still has the highest labor costs in the industry. Regardless, the UAW is propped up today by the Obama administration in a most unholy alliance that is funded by ordinary Americans.

Even in bankruptcy, GM is likely to need another bankruptcy because its biggest problems are unresolved. Like the crushing burden of public service unions on small government, the biggest financial issue that Government Motors faces is its enormous, and still growing, unfunded pension liability. When it first entered bankruptcy, its liability was over $100 billion and it was $20 billion behind on its payments. That is definitely not the way to run a sound company. It has not made great strides in paying off this debt.

You see, saving GM was not really the game. Obama had made Steve Rattner – "the Rat," as Stansberry calls him – "the crooked Democratic political operative under investigation for bribing New York State pension officials. Obama made him the 'car czar.' "Of course with Obama, all things are political and so, the Rat's job wasn't to fix GM. He was brought in to deliver mucho billions to the union and, this would be enough to deliver Michigan for Obama in the next election.

My point in bringing this in of course is that sometimes unions get too big for their breeches, and they must be stopped. Obama is not about to stop this major ally even though it hurts America, and Republicans are letting him do what he wants. In this case, the game was rigged and everybody lost except for the union that had put the company out of business in the first place. And, of course the government, well, at least the Democratic Party received some electoral spoils.

This is not a history book. It is intended to show Republican culpability in all that is wrong with America so that conservatives can make other plans. The reason, according to my thinking, is that Democrats have been so successful that Republicans choose to be inept. We call those kinds in our vernacular—wimps.

This is a book that hopes to titillate the senses of regular Americans so that we can check out how it is, and run that against how we think it ought to be in an honest life. Like most, I have incomplete knowledge about how the auto industry was from the Henry Ford Days when he was the CEO to when Barack Obama took over as Car America CEO in 2009, but it surely did not improve under Obama.

So, now that we got past that, let's take another look at the tough times that unions have created for regular businesses, such as mine, and of course the automobile industry in America. For the longest time, automobiles were a luxury item but eventually, they became a necessity for shopping and for finding the best entertainment within five miles—without having to hire a cab, and for taking nice vacations, etc.

We have already discussed a number of the most egregious offenses of car unions, in which the union leaders looked to take down the companies if they did not lift up the workers to the union cause.

Neither the public nor the government seemed to care. But, the entrepreneurs and investors cared because the union actions were a major detriment to the sustenance of the organization. With over 1000 entrepreneurial car manufactures now out of existence, unions have to take their share of the rap, and with that, their partners in crime, the Democrats deserve the other share.

Though my dad was a union guy, right or wrong, eventually he self-corrected. While still a union person, he invited me into his inner sanctum. He loved the Democratic Party. However, even my dad would not put up with the union members or their leaders ever doing anything that was against his system of beliefs.

As a Democrat, which I still am, and a person once sympathetic to unions, I found by working for IBM, a non-union company that when management treats employees right, unions are not needed. I still see conservatives being buffaloed by Democrats, and unions working against Republicans but I have yet to see an attempt at an effective response. Unfortunately for conservatives, somewhere in the recent past, Republicans changed from the "Party of "No," to the party of "whatever the Democrats want."

Ask yourself how over 1000 carmakers could go out of existence. Their products in most cases looked to be winners. To help you answer this for yourself, you might check out the Detroit marketplace from the early 1900's to see if you can discover a list of the defunct automobile manufacturers of the United States. Surely, the unions did not put them all out of business. But, they sure helped. I have done this work for you. You can get the complete list by taking below URL. Place it in your browser or type in the whole thing:

http://en.wikipedia.org/wiki/List_of_defunct_automobile_manuf acturers_of_the_United_States

Unions can be ruthless. Democrats can be ruthless. Republicans are wimps. A good counter strategy for conservatives to prevail cannot be to simply grin and bear it!

Chapter 8   Nostalgia Car Companies of Yesteryear

1000 Points of Light Eliminated

There is nothing nicer than a picture. There are a lot of nice pictures in this chapter. Another indisputable part of what is coming is that each and every auto maker highlighted in this chapter is out of business. They are gone. My suspicion, based on those smaller automobile companies that I was able to research is that they had to match the prevailing wage from the Detroit unions.

That would have been enough to put any lightly invested entrepreneurial company out of business. Can we ask for more proof than the fact that 1000 young companies disappeared completely and now we are stuck as Americans, as part owners of GM and Chrysler? Don't we all just love FORD for not taking the money?

The beauty of the brief expose over the last several chapters is coming to fruition below as we get a sample look at products that are unassailable in their uniqueness. However, each of the companies that made these machines banked on the principles of capitalism and investment to make them work.

Without the Internet, and television, these wonderful machines that I show you below from now defunct automobile makers could never have been made fully known to the vast American public.

So, let me ask again. Did the prevailing union wage put all of the thousands of companies shown at the URL in Chapter 7 out of business or was it that the market prevented them from being successful.

Think about this question while you take a break from hearing about the purposeful ineptness of the Republican Party. Enjoy the b/w car list and the great pictures courtesy of various sources on the Internet. If you are looking at the book via Kindle, then, the auto pictures below are in color. With Kindle, you can see how pretty and how manly these vehicles really are.

In the expose below, I will first show the company name, then the picture of the vehicle made by that company, and then under the picture, the name of the vehicle itself. Following this, there will be a brief write-up of the company. I can't wait to show you them. Here goes:

ALCO (1909–1913)

The Alco Company produced vehicles from 1909 through 1913, but they had been the American Locomotive Company from the early 1900's. At the time, they were the largest producer of steam locomotives in the world.

Cord (1929–1932,1936–1937)

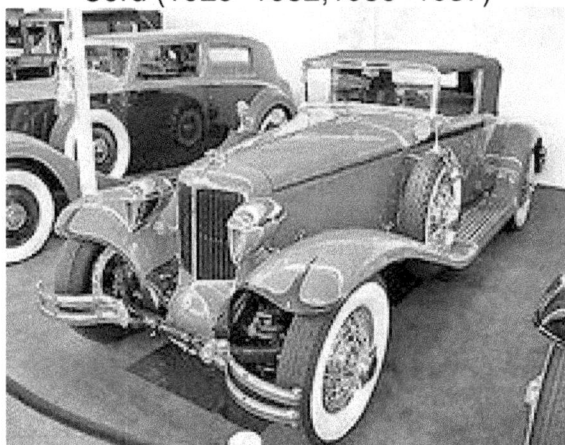

1930 Cord

Cord was the brand of an American company from Indiana, manufactured by the Auburn Automobile Company from 1929 through 1932 and again in 1936 and 1937. The Cord Corporation was founded and run by EL Cord as a holding company for his many transportation interests, including Auburn.

Duesenberg (1913–1937)

1930 Duesenberg

Founded in Des Moines, Iowa, United States by brothers August Duesenberg and Frederick Duesenberg, the company's principal place of operations moved to <u>Auburn</u>, <u>Indiana</u>. Duesenberg was active in various forms from 1913 to 1937.

Allstate (1952–1953)

1952 Allstate

The Allstate is a badge engineered version of the Henry J American automobile that was offered for sale through Sears, Roebuck during the 1952 and 1953 model years.

American Motors (or AMC) (1966–1987)

1974 AMC Gremlin

American Motors Corporation (AMC) was an American automobile company formed by the 1954 merger of Nash-Kelvinator Corporation and Hudson Motor Car Company. At the time, it was the largest corporate merger in U.S. history

Abbott-Detroit (1909–1916; Abbott 1917–1918)

1911 Abbot Detroit

Founded in 1909 in Detroit, the Abbott Motor Car Company and its successors were typical early manufacturers assembling purchased components like Continental engines in proprietary frames and bodies. In Abbotts case the formula proved to be successful, achieving some success in production car competition and producing just over 1,800 cars in 1912 while sustaining a more normal rate of 4-5 cars per working day (you didn't get Saturdays off in the Teens) for most of its life.

Auburn (1900–1936)

1932 Auburn S-100 A

The Auburn Automobile Company was founded in Auburn, Indiana, in 1875 by Charles Eckhart. Frank and Morris Eckhart's sons, began making automobiles, mixing two other local car manufacturers and moving into a larger plant in 1909. The company was forced to close activity during World War I.

The **AMC Eagle** was a compact-sized four-wheel drive passenger vehicle that was produced by American Motors Corporation (AMC). The AMC Eagle line of vehicles inaugurated a new product category of "sport-utility" or crossover SUV. Introduced in August 1979 for the 1980 model year, the coupe, sedan, and station wagon body styles were based on the AMC Concord.

Eagle (1988–1998)

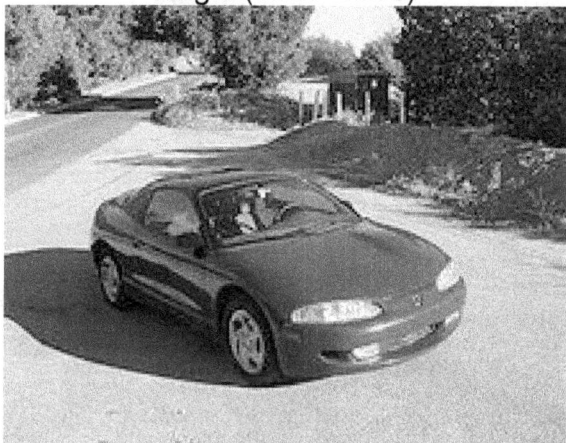

1995 Eagle Talon

The AMC Eagles were the only four-wheel-drive passenger cars produced in the U.S.[1] They were affordable cars offering a comfortable ride and handling on pavement together with superior traction in *light* off road use through AMC's innovative engineering and packaging.

E-M-F (1909–1912)

1912 EMF Model 30 Roadster

The E-M-F Company was an early American automobile manufacturer that produced automobiles from 1909 to 1912. The name E-M-F was gleaned from the initials of the three company founders: Barney Everitt (a custom auto-body builder from Detroit), William Metzger (formerly of Cadillac), and Walter Flanders (who had served as Henry Ford's production manager).

Graham-Paige (1928–1930; Graham 1930–1947)

1932 Graham Blue Streak

Graham-Paige was an American automobile manufacturer founded by brothers Joseph B. Graham (September 12, 1882–July 1970), Robert C. Graham (August 1885–October 3, 1967), and Ray A. Graham (May 28, 1887–August 13, 1932) in 1927. Automobile production ceased in 1940, and its automotive assets were acquired by Kaiser-Frazer in 1947. As a corporate entity, the Graham-Paige name continued until 1962. Isn't the Blue Streak worth a second look?

AM General -- The Hummer – (1992-) Well known by Americans

2010 Hummer H3

AM General introduced Hummer and later was taken over by GM. The brand was a casualty of government bailout of GM. The HUMVEE is still made by AM General. GM could not sustain its profits and make the H2, and H3 Hummer units. After not being able to sell the brand, GM, Government Motors, exited the marketplace.

Kaiser (1947–1955)

1954 Kaiser Darrin

Kaiser-Frazer Corporation's first car was launched for the 1947 model year. Known as the Kaiser Special, it was a four door sedan with a six cylinder engine. These two cars (with the Frazer) had the first true postwar sheet metal with enveloped bodies and fender lines that ran front to rear in an unbroken contour.

Nash (1917–1957)

1946 Nash 4-door Sedan

Nash Motors Company was an American automobile manufacturer based in Kenosha, Wisconsin, in the United States from 1916 to 1937. From 1937 to 1954, Nash Motors was the automotive division of the Nash-Kelvinator Corporation. Nash production continued from 1954 to 1957 after the creation of American Motors Corporation.

Nash pioneered unitary construction (1941), also a heating and ventilation system whose operating principles are now universally utilized (1938), seat belts (1950) and the manufacture of cars in the compact (1950), subcompact (1970) and muscle car (1957) categories. Look at that 1946 beauty! Would it not be nice to see them again?

Stout Scarab (1932–1946)

1935 Stout Scarab

The **Stout Scarab** is a unique 1930–1940s U.S automobile
designed by William Bushnell Stout and produced in small
numbers by Stout Engineering Laboratories and later by Stout
Motor Car Company of Detroit, Michigan.

Among a host of novelties and innovations, the Stout Scarab
is credited by some as the world's first
production minivan, and a 1946 experimental prototype of the
Scarab became the world's first car with a fiberglass body-
shell and air suspension. Can you imagine if these companies
still existed and their insights pushed the "Big Three" into
making cars for all tastes? I like the notion of the Stout Scarab
as a minivan. Cool!

Studebaker (1902–1963

1916 Studebaker

Besides the beautiful 1916 Studebaker shown above, the company had some other novel notions such as the Bullet Nose Models as shown below:

THE 1950 STUDEBAKER "BULLET NOSE" LAND CRUISER

Following the war, Studebaker introduced all-new styling for the 1947 model year and established itself as a styling leader. The 1950 models introduced the famous "bullet nose" styling, while 1951 marked the introduction of Studebaker's V8 engine.

International Harvester (1907–1975)

1978 International Harvester Scout II

The International Harvester Company (abbreviated
first IHC and later IH) today known as Navistar
International Corporation, was a United
States agricultural machinery, construction equipment, vehicle,
commercial truck, and household and commercial products
manufacturer.

In 1902, J.P. Morgan merged the McCormick Harvesting
Machine Company and Deering Harvester Company, along with
three smaller agricultural equipment firms, to form International
Harvester. International Harvester sold off its agricultural
division in 1985 and renamed itself Navistar
International Corporation in 1986. The Case IH brand began
when the IH agricultural division merged into J.I. Case.

Rambler (1900–1914)

1913 Rambler 5 Passengers

Rambler was an automobile brand name used by the Thomas B. Jeffery Company between 1900 and 1914, then by its successor, Nash Motors from 1950 to 1954, and finally by Nash's successor, American Motors Corporation from 1954 to 1969. It was often nicknamed the "Kenosha Cadillac" after its place of manufacture.

Rambler from Nash

Nash Rambler Almost beep beep

The **Nash Rambler** is a North American automobile that was produced by the Nash Motors division of Nash-Kelvinator Corporation from 1950 to 1954. On May 1, 1954, Nash-Kelvinator merged with the Hudson Motor Car Company to form American Motors Corporation (AMC). The Nash Rambler was then built by AMC in Kenosha, Wisconsin through 1955.

The Nash Rambler established a new segment in the automobile market and is widely acknowledged to be the first successful modern American compact car. Beep Beep!

The Little Nash Rambler – Subcompact Even Before Compact cars

"Beep Beep" is a song by The Playmates . The song describes a duel between the drivers of a Cadillac and a Nash Rambler on the road. The song was on the Billboard Top 40 charts for twelve weeks, and peaked at #20). The song sold over one million copies, and was awarded a gold disc. Concurrently with this song, American Motors (AMC) was setting production and sales records for the Rambler models. Look at that little guy. They were in driveways of my customers on my paper route.

The Playmates were a late 1950s vocal group, led by the pianist

Chic Hetti (born Carl Cicchetti, 26 February 1930), drummer; Donny Conn (born Donald Claps, 29 March 1930); and Morey Carr (born 31 July 1932), all from Waterbury, Connecticut. What a legacy!

Packard (1899–1958)

1951 Packard Convertible

Packard was an American luxury automobile marque built by the Packard Motor Car Company of Detroit, Michigan, and later by the Studebaker-Packard Corporation of South Bend, Indiana. The first Packard automobiles were produced in 1899, and the last in 1958

Willys 1908-1955

A classic Willys Jeep – the kind the Army used

Willys was the brand name used by Willys-Overland Motors, an American automobile company best known for its design and production of military Jeeps (MBs) and civilian versions (CJs) during the 20th century. Willys was bought by Kaiser and their name was changed in 1963.

Conclusion

There is no doubt about it. All of these innovative vehicles came from innovative companies who were put out of business by not being able to compete against the huge auto makers and the demand for a wage from huge unions that would put the companies out of business. None of these great cars and none of these great companies survived. Perhaps good leadership in Washington could have helped.

Chapter 9   Conservatives and Others Disgusted with the Republican Party?

Push me around Karl!

More and more conservatives are out and out disgusted with the Republican Party. Republican leadership, a.k.a. Karl Rove, and his boys (women need not apply), has somehow decided that conservatives are no longer worth their time. After all, conservatives come from all of Americana, both rural and urban, and few of the many are elite and even fewer are establishment.

Which conservative that you know likes to be pushed around the way Karl Rove likes to push US around? Who likes that kind of treatment from somebody who should be sucking up for our vote instead of reluctantly accepting it? Instead, the Republican leadership with Karl Rove as a de facto leader, having too much of a role, assures conservatives from all walks of life that the Republicans are too good for US! Conservatives do not measure up to the standards of Karl Rove and company, and Rove is convinced he can do better without US. Maybe the new Republican Hispanic / Latino initiative will fill the voter void. Maybe not! I am pleased that Rove is not with Trump like I am as if he were, I would have to second-guess myself.

Karl Rove may be the king of the Republicans, but he is not the king of conservatives. Take this story about conservative Representative Steven King as an example of Karl Rove, the absolute bully. King is one of my personal favorites in Congress and I see his perspective on the Karl Rove contingent just as

King does. Rove and company do not care at all about the conservative cause. King is no pushover and he is a great conservative, and a great legislator for the people.

King recognizes and speaks about the Karl Rove "war" on the Tea Party to fundraise, or to have any role in the Republican Party. Rove says "NYET." Conservatives need not apply. King doesn't turn the other cheek on Karl Rove.

King has no problem telling his supporters that "Nobody can bully me out of running for the U.S. Senate, not even Karl Rove and his hefty war chest." In the American Party which, I propose, certain people would be precluded from joining. Three of them are Karl Rove, John McCain, and Lindsey Graham. Others, such as real conservatives and folks like Steven King, in particular, will be welcome under the big tent of the American Party. I am sure you know that I speak clearly on behalf of conservatives with that pronouncement. RINOS are not welcome in the American Party, unless they first have a serious conversion and begin to love America.

You may know that Representative Steven King was a potential front-runner in the 2014 Republican primary to replace Sen. Tom Harkin, a Democrat from Iowa, who retired. King pulls no punches about how he was being attacked because Rove would rather anoint a Rovite RINO instead of a conservative with the guts to stand up for the good of America.

Back in 2013 King told supporters, as noted by the Des Moines Register, that "I'm under attack and I urgently need your help to fight back." He added that he had not made a decision about a run, "but already Karl Rove and his army have launched a crusade against me." Who is Karl Rove? He is everything about the Republican Party that conservatives cannot stand. John Galt certainly would not approve.

King continued: "I'm no stranger to outlandish attacks like this… they said I couldn't win in 2012— the entire political machine was against me— but I soundly defeated my opponent by 8 percentage points. So let me be clear. Nobody can bully me out of running for the U.S. Senate, not even Karl Rove and his hefty war chest."

As a pure conservative, I give Steven King a great Amen on that, and if I had my way, the Republicans should give the Karl a swift kick out the door.

So, here we are in 2016, wondering why Republicans are afraid of their shadow. After 2012, Fox fired Dick Morris, who is a reasonable man, and they kept Karl Rove. Karl Rove is afraid of his shadow but somehow he succeeds in having Republicans chasing their own tails. I am a very conservative Democrat. I do not want to join a Republican Party of gutless wimps and Roves. Back when Republicans stood for something, I actually considered it.

My desires are well known. I want US all to form an American Party with the name "The American Party." Can you think of a better name for Americans united for America? Who would not want to join?

Why should conservatives be forced to put up with fraidy cats, wimps, bohos and namby-pambies as representatives? What happened to guts and glory and for the greater good? You may recall that in 2010, many on the wrong side of history found themselves on the other side of the electorate. They got a one-way ticket home. The current crop of Republicans seems to have forgotten that the people do the ruling in America.

Back in 2010, conservatives were permitted to help the Republicans to kick the bad guys out of office so that a new batch of brave Republicans could storm in and prevent Obama from running away with America as he had done the previous two years. What happened to those guys? Did they lose their guts or just their conservative stripes? Why were they not brave enough to adhere to the principles that got them elected or at least tell us that they had abandoned them?

Conservatives always want the House of Representatives to act like men and we are not at all happy when they give the progressive liberals a break. We would also like the Senate to do the same, but we expect no consideration. The whole Senate must go other than Mike Lee and Ted Cruz. Even Pennsylvania's Pat Toomey went south on conservatives on gun control and is now likened to become the new Arlen Specter. He too must go.

Moreover, in 2016, Toomey is a worse choice than the Democrat McGinty. He is anti-Trump. I just sent the honorable Pat Toomey an email in which I congratulated him on his principled stance against Donald Trump. Toomey became a *Never Trumper*. I noted in my email to the Senator that I too am principled and because of my principles and his stance on my candidate, I am now a *Never Toomey* kind of guy.

Republicans and Democrats alike, who got to see the exit door close hand in 2010, thought then that their mission was to go along to get along despite the will of the people. If those days are back again, 2016 will find an army of RINOS wondering what happened. If they don't care if a Democrat is elected President, then in terms of sending back Republican sludge to Congress, I am fine with a Democrat.

In two years we'll make it right for Donald Trump but this time, we have some bad Republicans to involuntarily secede from the Senate and the House. Soon, as Trump begins his first term, there will be an initiative to form an American Party and in 2018, it will be a valid choice on the ballot, even though it will not fully blossom until 2020.

Conservatives are much better today for the 2010 reversal of power in the House. Yet, elites such as Karl Rove give no credit to conservatives who joined together under the TEA Party banner to defeat Democrats. One would conjecture that Rove would have preferred to deal with the Democrats than the conservatives in Congress, who now fill the aisles.

Despite an empty treasury, the Senate and the President never got the message of 2010 and Republicans apparently have become embarrassed in retrospect that they could not win without conservatives. They regret that in order to gain the House, they needed the good will of the TEA Party. To gain the Senate in 2014, they needed conservatives again.

Neither the Senate nor the President has made one initiative after the 2010 correction to help the American people confront the poor economy. Instead, unfortunately, Obama and company have stopped the pipeline; have cut back on oil leases on Public lands; and have added the most severe taxes of all time onto American businesses who choose to employ more than fifty people full-time. Is it no wonder that only by fudging the labor books, can the economy be made to look like it is surviving, though the lies are so big the administration suggests the economy is beginning to zoom. Hah!

What a shame for the Republican Party, the US Senate, and the worst President of all time. When will they ever learn? The Democrats are still in give-away mode, and a number of Republicans are now mumbling like redistribution and the rest of the Democratic platform is their new enlightenment. Some are wondering why the give-away sign-up sheet is not on the Republicans side of the aisle. This must cost them their jobs.

The Senate and the President are busy getting the stuff ready for the next great Democrat give-away. This was promised to the "47%" during the 2012 election season. Dumass Americans bought all the Democratic rhetoric. It seems they checked their brains at the womb.

Rush Limbaugh appropriately calls these dumass Americans who voted for their stomachs instead of for the country, *low information voters*. So now the Democrats must pay up with some shekels from the US Treasury. How soon good people forget!

Obama initially tricked millions of Americans into thinking he is the real savior. In his first four years, he proved to the thinking world that he is nobody's savior. In fact, after eight years now, many pundits, who have a relationship with the truth, have him pegged as the front runner for the title of worst President of all-time.

Until now, it had been the only honor bestowed on Jimmy Carter in his lifetime. Carter may take issue with Obama winning the award. Despite the truth, dumass Americans remained unaware as they waited for their share of Obama's stash. They are the low-information voters by choice, and they are sinking America fast. Wake up guys!

Because they chose not to know, dumass Americans re-anointed Barack Obama, as their savior in chief in 2012. The last thing conservatives need now is for Republican legislators to become infatuated with the supposed "great one." One Democratic Party is much more than enough for any country. Must Republicans become Democrat-lite to appease those in their party that have disdain for conservatives?

If Republican legislators choose to go along with the Democrats just to get their names on all of the give-away stuff, then, just like in 2010 and 2014, when 2016 rolls along, conservative voters must send these charlatans back home. When they get home, the folks who they betrayed (US) should not be offering any welcome home parades for their poor service.

Ask "Mr. Pro-life," himself, Bart Stupak a bad name from the corrupt past, what it is like to trick your constituency. You get one chance and then you are o-u-t. Mr. Stupak is now a lobbyist, the lowest form of occupation in the US. He deserves it!

Democracy, Republic, and Constitution are important civics terms that we learned in grade school. In many ways, they describe our founder's America. Our President for the last eight years seemed to hold none of these terms in high regard. So, it is up to conservatives to make sure our country exists for the long haul with our founders' attributes. Donald Trump is the only person on the horizon promising a good life in America who actually knows how to deliver. Trump is a winner, not a loser.

We cannot depend upon low-information Republican legislators. That means that conservatives in Congress must stop Democrats and the President, who are hell bent on compromising our nation by giveaways, deficits, debt, runaway immigration, and healthcare at the third world level. It may be too late for Obama and never should Hillary be considered. Trump will stop the Democrats and move our nation in the correct direction. Meanwhile, we can work on creating the American Party.

If Republicans could see the light, then, just like Johnny Cash, [I saw the light!] that would be really nice. However, I see seven thousand Karl Rove's and no Ronald Reagan's. What do you see? I think that in their arrogance, Republicans would prefer to turn Johnny Cash's lights out on conservatives.

Our wonderful America was never guaranteed to continue, even when past leaders held tightly to the founders' principles. Chances of an America that continues for many more years have been lessened substantially after the last election by a President with little regard for America or Americans.

It has been lessened even further as Republicans who have begun to publicly denigrate conservatives. This year, Republican establishment elites actually have chosen to denigrate the nominee for President who represents their Party. Time to purge the sludge from the Party. Why would the Party of Lincoln not try for a better America by working with Donald Trump, the best thing to come along in an awful long time?

Many conservatives fear that Barack Obama as a socialist / progressive has had a major interest in moving the US from capitalism to a more "sharing" type of government form. He has just months left but every day we find out he has done something that had been hidden previously. Who knows all of what Obama has done to harm America?

Communism is an option for Obama. Since he was reared in a family of communists (mother, father, grandmother, grandfather on mother's side), and many of his "friends," are avowed communists, the President may very well be a communist also but we'll stop short of calling him that.

However, when it looks, smells and then it tastes like it, it typically is it. If Obama is not a communist, he sure looks like one. In all cases, he is an avowed fascist and socialist and has no business being the President of capitalist America.

A progressive socialist is far enough off the founders' notions of good government that it is not safe for any American to trust that this President will do the right thing for America or Americans—ever. We can say the same for his anointed successor, Hillary Clinton.

I'll let others determine whether this President is a communist or not. In the meantime, I will hold onto the few possessions that I have since I surely do not trust the Obama administration to take care of anything of mine that I hold dear.

And, so, in this time of Obama socialism, it is strange indeed for Republicans to be quiet about the poor job Obama has been doing for the country as he attacks all conservative values including religious freedom. It is even stranger that the Republicans would rather fight their conservative base than Obama. And, so, conservatives must fight back. The American Party is our best option. What American besides Obama and Hillary Clinton can be against the American Party?

With America originally being formed as a mercantilist economy, a form of capitalism in which the invisible hand is much more visible, a move to full socialism or even to communism would be like nothing Americans would want to imagine.

As I read my own words, I ask why is it that Republicans have not cautioned Americans about where Obama has been taking US. Have Republicans become Democrats without the name? America survived for well over 100 years very successfully before mercantilism changed to pure capitalism with the introduction of the Personal Income Tax in the early 1900's. Who in their right mind on April 15th ever applauds the day the Personal Income Tax took effect under Woodrow Wilson?

Isn't it amazing that the US got along for so long without the Democratic Party's notion of personal and corporate income taxation that could would swell government coffers enough to be able to be used for redistribution? Thank you President Wilson. You were the first purely progressive President. Thank you so much for giving US citizens the IRS.

One thing few are denying in 2016, no matter what you want to call it, at the end of this term, Obama will have taken the nation closer to socialism from capitalism than any President ever before—even Wilson.

Perhaps even the name America is not secure. Perhaps you too have seen ads by investment companies exhorting Americans to buy gold while referencing how bad things will be in Obama's third term. That sure is a spooky thought. In Barack Obama's sixth term, however, it would be time for the Obama loyalists to suggest that the name America should be changed for the "better."

You may recall that even Bedford Falls accepted corruption as a way of life when George Bailey could no longer keep it straight. Then, Potter changed its name to Pottersville in the hit movie, "It's a Wonderful Life." So, all bets for a name change for America are still on, especially in a sixth Obama term. Can it happen? Will Republicans stand up for Americans and use conservatives to help rather than cast conservative overtures aside? Or will it be a job left to the American Party?

Perhaps in a sixth term, our beloved America, with Obama hanging on as President, might be renamed Obamaville. If so, it could happen in the second edition of the Roaring Twenties sometime after 2020. It seems this same story about good triumphing over evil after monumental setbacks has been played out many times throughout history even long before Frank Capra wrote about good and bad people in his epoch 20th century movie.

I ask myself sometimes if our Constitutional Republic can withstand all of the challenges required to adapt to this strange and corrupt 21st century. And so, if it cannot, the logical choice in the sixth term of Obama would be to bring on the United States of Obamaville. I know that I am not laughing about the prospects of that becoming a reality, but I am sure many dumass Americans, or as Limbaugh calls them, "low information voters," who are eternally loyal to the Obama cause, would think it is a "cute" idea.

If all of this sounds sick but not so far-fetched, then eliminate Obama's sixth term in 2016 and vote for a real man, Donald Trump.

Chapter 10   Can America Survive Democrats w/o "R" Opposition?

Should Republicans implicitly trust President Obama?

Scholars from the past have offered many opinions about many different types of governments and their propensities to survive for more than 200 years. Democracies typically do not have the staying power that we have witnessed in our Constitutional Republic, which we enjoy calling The United States of America.

Conservatives wonder why, when the stakes are so high, that President Obama would be leading us in the wrong direction, despite warnings from the present, and from the past. We would all like to trust the Obama regime for our future but can we? Would it work out well for US or would we be like the proletariat in communist Russia? The President is just too good at the art of prevarication to trust, and the Republicans have not been prepared to counter his lies with the truth—the best form of resistance. Is it no wonder that conservatives are in a deep conundrum?

From observing and analyzing his first term, many saw the Obama way in *term two* as a quick path to perdition. It is almost complete and we are much closer to perdition but somehow America was a tougher nut for the communist Obama to overtake.

If Barack Obama were Rhett Butler, I would expect that any day we would hear from the White House: *Quite frankly America, I don't give a damn!* But, for me and many other conservatives, it would not be news. It would mean we had to act decisively— even faster than our intuitions had suspected.

As this book continues, we will take a peek at some of the foreboding cautions about a disappearing America brought to us by the ghosts of the present and the past. For now, we know that Obama is about gone and his vision for the next four years is Hillary Clinton and whether Hillary gets to be in charge is singularly up to Ebenezer Obama and the instrumentals will be played by a new group in town, "The Get-Along Republicans."

For conservatives, that is quite a chilling thought. In fact, it is too chilling to not look for relief. Neither Republicans nor Obama give a damn about conservatives. It would be better for all conservatives to understand that sooner than later.

And so, now more than ever, the once loyal conservative constituents see no reason for conservative legislators in Congress to cave to any Obama thought. It was not the progressives that put our conservative lawmakers in office. It was US.

And, so it is time that these Republicans recognize that an electorate espousing conservative values is the reason they got to serve America for even one term. It would be a real shame for any conservative legislator who leans Democrat to have to get a new job in just a few years. But, it would be a just reward for poor services rendered.

Is America Finished?

Words from people in the past and present often help us in forming our perspectives. Each of the quoted phrases shown after the few stories that are coming, offers a unique perspective and a unique way with words about the tentative nature of all governments, especially, a semi-democracy such as ours.

As many already know, it is unusual for any form of government to last more than 200 years in practice. With that knowledge, all Americans that are dedicated to America should be very concerned. The US is well over 200 years into the same governmental form. A vigilant nation would take notice.

As a final thought before the quoted piece, I would bet that if we asked the Roman people, after their own historical comeuppance, whether they were really prepared to give up their empire and their lifestyle, and their homes, for something they did not bring upon themselves, the answer would be a flat "NO!"

As history shows us, the Roman leaders ran a great empire; however they got stretched thin with warring and entanglements in many countries. Even though none of the Caesars ever went on an apology tour across the various countries in the Empire, lots of citizens of lots of non-Roman countries did not like the Romans. There are some parallels with America but not with its current leader. Romans always were tough while they were awake and not drunk with booze, typically fine wine served in pewter goblets.

Eventually, many smaller nations and tribes figured out where the Romans were vulnerable and they proceeded to pick apart the Roman Empire in the same fashion that a school of piranha picks on a live corpse.

For a mental visualization of the beginning stage, think about how beautiful a whale in the sea is to observe, especially when it comes up, dips down and makes that beautiful splash. Then, think about all those bites and nips and rips that you see in this magnificent animal's tail fin. This is the norm of the sea as many sea animals enjoy getting a little chunk from the whale's tail, even if they are not attacking its life per se.

But, when the tail completely disappears from too many bites, perhaps from a sustained attack from a school of nasty little fish, or from one bite too many over time, and the whale begins to run for its life—this better describes the plight of the Romans. It also describes all of the other empires that temporarily ruled others. Eventually, all the big empires went down from little nips. Their tails eventually disappeared and they could no longer get out of Dodge. They drowned in their own incompetence.

For our edification on this analogy, it helps to know that smaller sea predators will often attack the tail of a whale that they are hunting. Think of this in the same way as the small tribes pecking away at the flanks of the Roman Empire, and the representatives of *dumass* America, and the President pecking away at the fundamentals of our Constitution.

Predators nip and bite the pectoral fins and the tail of the whale hoping to immobilize it. With persistence, and avoiding the big whale swallow, their attacks will damage those parts of the whale so significantly that unless it can quickly swim away from the attack, it will never again be able to swim. When a whale cannot swim it is like a human that cannot swim—the whale will drown because as we all know, it is not a fish. A recently dead whale feeds a lot of nasty little fish.

The way I see it, with President Obama looking to sell America to the lowest bidder; the quotes below have even more meaning. However, *dumass* Americans, or as Rush Limbaugh calls them, "*low information voters,*" won't really get the meaning of these quotes unless and until they feel similar pain to the contributors in their own lives.

The Romans needed to feel pain before they realized they needed to come back to attention. If they had felt pain sooner than later, they may have adjusted and survived the attacks. They did not, and that is why Rome is not a superpower today. Will the US have a similar fate?

Check out these great words from figures from the past and a few great figures from today:

"I do not know if the people of the United States would vote for superior men if they ran for office, but there can be no doubt that such men do not run." – Alexis de Tocqueville

" I think Donald Trump will be regarded in history as one of the superior men of which de Toqueville speaks." – Brian W. Kelly, your author

"Democracy is a pathetic belief in the collective wisdom of individual ignorance." – H.L. Mencken

"The human race is so obviously imperfect that man could not possibly have been the creation of an omnipotent God, but—at best—the bungled effort of 'an incompetent committee of gods.' " – H.L. Mencken

While I was musing about the Obama victory in November 2012, I discovered a lot of others, who felt just as dejected as I. One of those was a man, very much disappointed with President Barack Obama's winning. He gave a message to the nation. Here is his message, as delivered on a social media forum. A few others follow this:

"Goodluk America u just voted for economic & spiritual suicide. Soulless fools….What subhuman varmint believes others must pay for their obesity booze cell phones birth control abortions & lives?" – Ted Nugent

"Many Israeli officials expressed disappointment with Obama's re-election." – *Israel Today Magazine*

"America has died... can't stop crying... thanks a lot Christians, for not showing up. You disgust me." – Victoria Jackson, Former *Saturday Night Live* star, post-election

"...HIS chosen ones (if you know what I'm talking about) will simply jump the borders, come here for free medical care, social security to which they are NOT entitled, and so on and so on..... Read between the lines America....You helped to screw all the good people & played into the hands of a crafty potter............'Nuff said." – Auntie Digri

"Our country is now in serious and unprecedented trouble... like never before," – Donald Trump

Hey where did Trump come from here in this book? The fact is that "the Donald" has been helping America form a proper perspective on reality and government for a long time. This quote was from 2012 when Obama won the presidency for the second time. Trump lamented because he is for America first!

Conservatives were heartbroken with the election results, and still feel due our righteous indignation at what *dumass* Americans [a.k.a. low information voters] brought upon us. With fifty-nine precincts in Philadelphia showing zero votes for Romney, it makes one think about whether we are all in some game, playing the parts of unique chess pieces on a board meant to frustrate the human mind.

Yet, as conservatives, our one time allies in the fight against progressivism, the *Republicans,* continually have chosen to remain silent against election fraud, and anything else that they were sent to Congress to prevent. Now, they have decided they want to placate illegal aliens and Hispanics rather than embrace their one-time conservative base. Conservatives will last forever but Republicans will go the way of the ~~Wimps~~ Whigs!

Chapter 11   Can Republicans Prosper as Democrat Lite?

Booker T Could Help Obama

It is a somewhat new phenomenon that the leadership of the Democratic Party, in fact any political party from any country, finds its success in pyrrhic victories for the Party, rather than real victories for the people that they represent. Perhaps one day, somebody in this President's inner circle will explain economics to the President as he does not understand that without successful businesses, there can be no job growth. A course in ECON 101 would go a long way at the White House. As long as the course was marked on a curve, even Obama would have a chance of passing.

President Obama does not really have a business advisor or a good man or woman upon whose shoulder he can lean. It would be nice if a great teacher like Booker T. Washington were alive again today to help guide this President. Mr. Washington once schooled the most powerful Presidents. Booker T. Washington was simply the best at what he did. He was a teacher of presidents.

With respect to the office of the president today, I regret to posit that if Booker T. Washington were alive, he too would get the short shrift from the Messiah. Our President unfortunately would treat this great man the same way that he treats other great men, such as the inimitable Ambassador Alan Keyes or the new good-guy in America, Dr. Benjamin Carson. Obama thinks more of Obama than he does about getting it right for Americans, and so he asks for no help though it would be freely given, and it is sorely needed. Can the fact that he loves Hillary Clinton be a notion in the same vein?

Booker T. Washington once said that: "Success is to be measured not so much by the position that one has reached in life as by the obstacles which he has overcome." Whether in business or life, there's a fine line between success and failure. Booker T. Washington's quote highlights the inevitability of obstacles on the path to success. Barack Obama, who achieved Community Organizer as a strata in life before politics, does not understand the notion of real success. Mr. Obama does understand the notion of winning and being worshipped for winning while losers get the weeping and the gnashing of teeth, and are dismissed as failures in society.

If Obama ever accepted a loss gracefully, he would be begging both Alan Keyes and Dr. Benjamin Carson into his inner circle of advisors. Then again, Obama takes no advice. Booker T. Washington, who advised American Presidents at the turn to the 20th century, would serve no purpose in an administration in which the President had received all of his instructions directly from God or another almost-as-powerful spirit, since Obama is his own personal Messiah. The man who knows everything requires no input—no advice.

Success and failure go hand-in-hand. Those looking to succeed must first fail or learn from those who have failed before them. Our President does not see it this way. His handlers have yet to permit him to admit to failing, and so our President believes he has never failed. Yes, Virginia, such humungous egos do exist.

Now that the last big election for the "Messiah" is well in even his past, all conservatives need to come to grips with the fact that we lost. This guy won! How?

Republicans for their part, have to decide whether conservatives are even worth their time. Democrats see this travesty as a huge win for them. They think that just like 2008, they are in the catbird's seat. Conservatives, at least those not bound and gagged by the Republican Party say: "No way Jose!" However, it is not really the Democrats that conservatives are most worried about in 2013/2014.

Wimpy, gutless, spineless Republican lawmakers as noted in other parts of this book have basically given it all up because Obama might have been upset if they did not. The Republicans were very concerned that the size of their shrimp at the Democrat socials would be reduced if they did not play ball.

Real conservatives are not ready to give two cents for what Obama thinks. Yet, the rhetoric since the 2012 election from House and Senate Republicans showed far too strong a desire to become the winning team by emulating the philosophies of the winning team—the Democrats.

News channels report of anxious Republicans with quivering voices making overtures to get along and crawl across the aisle for a small favor, or God willing, to receive just a good word from a friendly Democrat. Conservatives want none of that.

I am unaware of any conservative overture towards Republican legislators advising them that it is now their job to be more like the Democrats? Au contraire! Republican leaders, however, all on their own, are ready to fire their conservative base, especially TEA Party advocates.

Republicans have had a big drink of the Kool-Aid and now believe what the corrupt press says is keeping them down. Will Republicans tell conservatives to take a hike? In many ways, they have done so already. After all, conservatives were not able to elect them a Republican President. Then again, neither was the great "Karl Rove."

I cannot see even dumass Democrats opting to vote for the Republican side even if the Party of Lincoln declares itself the new and improved party of giveaways—even if Lincoln himself would be their next candidate! I cannot see even Hispanics and Latinos opting to vote for the Republican side even if the Party of Lincoln declares itself the most welcoming party for those from south of the border. There is something about telling the truth that comes before all of this.

Logic dictates that a bidding war for grabby and needy constituents will never be won by Republicans. So, any overtures to dumass Democrats or the Hispanic / Latino community from Republicans will not amount to anything worthwhile—but don't tell Karl Rove that!

For the heck of it, let's see what a few preemptive strikes v conservatives from Republicans might look like. If they are so fed up with conservatives, Republican strategists might deploy any number of grab-bag programs to gain the votes of non-conservatives. I have a number of thoughts on what the Republicans can put on the table if they opt to engage in a bidding war against the Democrats in future elections to gain their constituents. Don't get upset with me. Please! This is for demonstration purposes only!

How about increasing the immigration limit just for Hispanics? An even sweeter deal would be to declare a five-year moratorium on immigration from any traditional nation, such as Ireland, France, England, Uganda, Russia, Egypt, and all others. Only Hispanics and Latinos would be eligible for citizenship in this sweet deal. Surely by bringing forth such a proposal, Hispanics and Latinos would then know for sure that Republicans love them the best and Republicans, not Democrats would gain their vote.

Can it be however, that regular Americans do not care whether Republicans or Democrats win elections as long as the right platform is put forth? I do not care whether the R or D party is victorious if the set of intentions for the party is conservative. I do not trust the D party at all and now I do not trust the R Party. So, it really is time to bring on the American Party. A Johnny Carson game show could be built called "Who do you trust?" if it had not already been a stop on Carson's road to the Tonight Show.

Back to the moratorium! How about if the moratorium lasts until all of the willing residents of Mexico and Latin America are completely unpacked and are living in the US as citizens. To make it easier, the US government can totally eliminate those silly loyalty tests and the oath of allegiance for Hispanics and Latinos. Shouldn't such a magnanimous gesture be more than enough to gain at least 90% of the Hispanic vote for Republicans?

Republicans can come up with something even bigger than citizenship with a bit more creativity. If Republicans think the problem they are having is because they are not nice enough to a constituency today owned by the Democratic party, trying to buy some votes from this community may work a little bit, but it will not make up for all of the conservatives the Republican party will lose.

There can be such a pile of benefits to Hispanics who choose to convert to Republican that in no way could Democrats ever match such a generous Republican program. It could help the GOP win many future elections by robbing our US Treasury for the benefit of its new constituency—Hispanics. Regardless of its impact on the country and its impact on our ability to balance our budget, deals could be made that would permit Latinos and Hispanics to stay in their home countries and they would still be able to collect major stipends from dumass American gringos taxpayers, who would not know what hit them.

The objective of the "Beat the Democrats on Giveaways Program," would always have to be kept on the front burner at all times. The consultants have long concluded that Republicans got beat by Hispanics and Latinos who were simply not interested in their spiel. Therefore, the program objective, of course, would be to suck up to these constituencies in whatever ways are possible.

In this way, all Hispanics and Latinos, both citizens and non-citizens living in any part of the Americas would be included in this magnificent largesse from the US Treasury—but this time it would be sponsored by the Republicans.

This would surely be a Santa Claus moment? Meanwhile the conservatives would be out forming the American Party as this would surely show US that Republicans had gone mad.

Chapter 12   Can Anybody Beat Santa Claus?

Will The Thomas Mara Party ever win?

Rush Limbaugh, a leading conservative is correct that "it is practically impossible to beat Santa Claus." Unknowingly with this statement, Limbaugh has given the Democrats a winning all-purpose mantra: "Republicans want to take away Santa Claus."

The Democrats well know that the secret to continually winning elections is to make sure your Party is the one viewed as Santa Claus, and the other Party is portrayed as District Attorney Thomas Mara as in The Miracle on 34th St.

Knowing this, one would believe that a group of theoretically intelligent Republicans, with well-paid leadership at the Party level, would be able to enlist a Madison Avenue image firm to rid them of the label, "The Thomas Mara Party."

If you know your enemy and you know the shape of the grenades they throw and you know when they are going to throw them, you ought to be able to do something about not getting hit by them. Perhaps you can throw a few back and cause some damage. That is, if you are not a Wimp and if you care enough to make an effort. What is wrong with Republicans anyway?

During this expose on Democrats, we took the argument against Republicans becoming the stuff-meisters ad absurdum to show how nobody can out "give-away" the Democrats. The exercise demonstrates quite vividly how stupid trying to out-bid the Democrats on stuff would be. Nobody can give away more stuff to people who not need it than the Democrats. That is a certainty!

Unfortunately, there are those in the Republican Party, many of whom are in the Congress, who at this very moment are trying to figure out how to make deals just as stupid. They are looking for any way they can to look weak and make it seem like the devil made them do it.

They appear to think that they have received a secret message from conservatives, telling them to kneel down on the other side of the aisle and offer bigger grab-bags and bigger concessions than the Democrats. Conservatives that I know swear that they did not send that message.

From being a non-voting Kennedy Democrat in my teens (too young), I have come to believe in the principles of conservatives. According to today's standards, Kennedy was a conservative. Yet, I continue to admire the tenacity of the Democrats. They do not die when clearly killed.

I do not however, find any solace in the ideology of the Democratic Party leaders. The Democrats fight hard to avoid any loss, whereas the Republicans unfortunately, are Wimps, ever ready to give it up and abandon their own principles when the going gets tough. Conservatives are really sick of that. We deserve better, and the American Party is an avenue to give us a way to end such absurdity.

Obviously, pandering to any part of the US citizenry is not the way to go for Republicans as the minuses far outweigh the plusses. Permitting taxes to be raised without going off the fiscal cliff likewise has no advantages for the conservative cause. It has no advantages for America either!

My sincere apologies to all Latinos and Hispanics! I hit you all pretty hard in my give-away for demonstration purposes only... Latinos / Hispanics and Irish and anybody else with a life to live must work hard to become good Americans. Good Americans are all I care about in this book. Republicans are teetering on being excommunicated from the term "Good Americans."

Anybody paying attention to the news in the post-2012-election period saw that there was a lot of rhetoric about stuff supposedly needed to attract the Hispanic / Latino vote. And, so the analysis and the accusations about Republicans ready to give up conservatives for Hispanics does have substantial validity. Republicans would give up conservatives in a split second if they thought they could gain Hispanics into the fold, regardless of their inbred ideologies. The argument, though preposterous, has validity.

Giving stuff to any constituency to get their vote, however, is a sham. Yet, the Democrats have tried their hand in such sordid systems for years, and they have been exceedingly successful. Why? It is because a large part of their constituency consists of dumass Americans, so aptly labeled as low information voters by Rush Limbaugh. The palms of their hands are always sunburned.

In the 2012 election, Democrats sure found a way to offer every identifiable minority, including women, who are actually a majority, some specific stuff to get their vote. Democrats are great campaigners for sure. Obama himself is the greatest campaigner of all time other than Bill Clinton. Honesty is not a necessary ingredient to a successful Democratic campaign.

Obama needed plenty of time to get his message across again and again and again and again. He does have the bully pulpit and a complicit media that choose not to be the fourth estate. Bill Clinton was not like Obama but he reached for the same trite goals. As an orator for Democrats, he was much more succinct and pithy than Obama and he was always able to get his message across without ever needing an "again."

From the results of the 2012 election, it sure looks like the stuff idea worked for Democrats. Republicans, to their credit, did not play that game in the last election. Some analysts say it cost them the election. Those analysts are wrong. Unfortunately, Republicans seem to buy the whole post-election consulting analysis. Real conservatives think we have a better and a bigger message for Americans who really like America. It is simple. Let's get back to having a great country by electing competent leaders! Let's start with Donald Trump.

Democrats, dumass Americans, and low-information voters need to be more concerned about America than another Democrat election victory as their families more than any others will be affected.

If we get into an open bidding war in the future for voters; it will be a shame for America. It will be a hopeless system for our children and our children's children. In such a system, there would be no need to have any debates or discuss issues or matters of national importance as none of that would matter.

Who would care about our America, the good ole US of A, if the payoff for the individual was big enough? Who would really care about this country if both Republicans and Democrats created a bunch of prostitute voters on the take?

Santa won the last election

But, if it were Santa Claus's big bag from which the gifts emanated, maybe it could be excused? I don't think so but then again, Republicans lost the last election.

Chapter 13 Republicans and Conservatives Have Lost Commonality

Is the Divorce final?

How much do conservatives have in common with the Republicans of today? The fact that the question is put forth begs the response: "Not much!" Conservatives are not about to negotiate limits to our freedom by changing the bill of rights to give government more power, even if it upsets our one time allies, the Republicans and their friends the RINOS. Why would any American want to relinquish individual freedom to a tyrannical government wanting to keep Americans under its control? I hope I do not have to answer that!

In his well-publicized interview in summer 2013 with Greta Van Susteren of Fox News Rush Limbaugh acknowledged the rift between conservatives and Republicans but he sees it as something even larger. He sees the Republicans and Democrats becoming like-minded almost like there is now just one Party. Here is Rush in his own words:

"And I don't think it's so much conservative versus liberal, although it is, but it's Washington versus the rest of the country is what's really transpiring now. And Washington has a mindset and a desire for the country that doesn't dovetail with the majority of the American people."

Though Rush Limbaugh, the true voice of conservatism in America today, does not think that a new party would help matters right now, he is not totally against it. He thinks it would be better for conservatives to fight for and win the leadership positions in the Republican Party and make it the party for conservatives. Let the RINOS find another Party. If that can work, then it should be tried but like Rush, I would not expect the Republicans and all of their power and money to cede anything to conservatives.

Thus, the talk about forming the American Party is long overdue as conservatives are getting hammered by Republicans at every turn, and there are no doors opening for conservatives to have a larger voice in Party decisions. It took a billionaire, Donald Trump to crash through the elite establishment barrier to be in a position to represent the real people in this country instead of the power brokers and political donors. Thank God for that!

The TEA Party was rendered mostly ineffective by the mainstream media with their reputation-destroying attacks on Sarah Palin along with Karl Rove's disdain for non-elite conservatives. It still exists but has been muted. The moms and dads and uncles and aunts who once tuned in as silent members of the TEA Party are still very upset and instead of joining anything, they are voting at a strong level to effect change. Donald Trump did not just happen. It is grassroots conservatives, populists, and nationalists—those who love America who brought him the nomination.

When the American Party is brought forth, it will take 99% of Republicans, many Democrats, and most Independents. The TEA Party that is left at that time must listen to Americans. It must permit itself to be quickly absorbed by the American Party.

In fact, I would suspect that some important American Party leaders will come from the TEA Party. Perhaps a candidate for President from the American Party will show up from the TEA Party to help us all create the American Party that we all desire, and one that will succeed!

The Republican Party has stood for over 150 years from when we conservatives abandoned the Whigs and the intrinsic evil that they promulgated. Republicans began their success by getting Abraham Lincoln elected as the President of the USA.

Lincoln ultimately preserved the Union and freed men and women of color from the bondage of slavery. The reasons why this Party wants to purge conservatives are not fully understood and it is not within its founding. It was a great party in the mid 1900's. The Republican Party is now an unfortunate reincarnation of the Whig Party with a leaning towards progressivism. It has lost its value to regular Americans who love America and especially conservatives.

The facts are clear that John McCain, Lyndsey Graham, Karl Rove and other elite RINOS from the Republican Party cannot be entrusted to preserve conservative values. They prove it every day. How can we conservatives work with people who are not really on our side?

They have sold out conservative principles for the comfort of getting along with the person across the aisle and the Washington lobbyists and the elite Republicans. They do not value the existence of conservatives in the Party and are giving US less and less voice.

Will they drink the tonic of conservatism again and be cured. Don't hold your breath! Republicans will go the way of the Whigs when left without conservatives. My prediction is that these elites may become powerful members of the Democratic Party. Good riddance!

A number of years ago I was puzzled that so many conservatives of small means were members of the Republican Party, the traditional party of big business and industry. It made little sense to me at a dollars and cents level. Before the open emergence of a left wing of elite establishment types in leadership positions of the Republican Party. Even now, I saw regular Americans signing out from the Democratic Party and their raunchy liberalism and signing up with the clean, better living, better ethics, better morals of conservative Republicans.

They were becoming conservatives and the Republicans were the most convenient Party to accept their views on life. Republicans unfortunately are no longer there.

I ask myself as a Democrat, what is a real Republican – one who has the power to influence the Party? None of my friends working in sweat shops or in menial white collar jobs fit the bill. As I thought it through, I saw Republicans running small businesses and large businesses with great success. Yet, I wondered about the small business owners with just about $1million in assets as to how influential even they could be in the money-rich Republican Party at the National Level.

So, I took a stab at it. I defined a Republican as someone with over $50 million in wealth who wants more, and who has some means to achieve it that depends often on positive government policy. These real Republicans do need the willingness of the little conservatives to both fund their political aspirations and to provide votes, which they would not otherwise get because their true numbers are very small. That's really about it.

So, now, it seems that Republicans think they can do their magic without having the conservative values that attract the small time voters such as me. Many of my Democrat friends and relatives recently joined the Republican Party but not for its values. They joined so that they could vote for Trump in the 2016 Primary Election. I am glad they did but they are volatile Republicans at best and would leave in a heartbeat to join the American Party when it comes.

The GOP elites would be happy of course if I would simply agree to vote for them no matter what their platform might be, and I would permit them to take a bit of my money for their cause. I always wondered why that worked and I think it is because most people who want to be good people are in fact conservatives. Don't tell that to a liberal—but it is the truth.

Unfortunately, Republicans are messing up their deal with the little people. The new mantra of the RINO Republicans who control the Party today is to become chummy with the big government Left. This will not work because the small time conservatives they leave behind are not low-information voters – just the opposite. They are high information voters, and they will leave the Republican Party as soon as they see that it has sold them out.

The GOP is gone for good. It is difficult to believe; but it is true. There is no reason for conservatives to stick around and support a GOP elite leadership that plans to sell us all and our posterity back into thralldom. To the logical conservative mind, it is far more advantageous for the furthering of the conservative cause to form a workable third party?

There should be more options on the table than the tyranny-lite that the Republicans are peddling nowadays. The American Party offers hope for a really exciting and productive future for conservatives and for all Americans of good will.

May God give US our opportunity!

Chapter 14 The American Party—A New Conservative / Nationalist Party!

The Conservative/ Nationalist Party?

At the present time, there is no national conservative party per se but politically independent Sean Hannity is a registered member of the Conservative Party of New York. Hannity quit the Republican Party about ten years back because he is a conservative and he was disgusted with the McCain presidential campaign. He saw gentleman John McCain and other RINO Republicans taking control of the Republican Party and it did not look well for conservatives.

The new American Party will take just about all conservatives, nationalists, and populists as well as those from other parties that are fed up with the status quo. Obama and Hillary love the status quo and that provides even more impetus for the American Party with Donald Trump as President.

The American Party will be the largest party ever and it will bring a great America back to all of us. It will be the party of America for Americans. For purposes of this chapter in *Kill the Republican Party,* when we say conservative or nationalist or populist or America lover, we mean all types of potential new members of the American Party.

From my perspective, the Conservative Party would not be a good name for recruiting conservative Democrats, Libertarians, Constitutionals, Greens, and conservative Republicans. It would appear to be a face lift to the Republican Party. The name American Party cannot be argued with. It is the Party for America and Americans. It will draw conservatives from the Republican Party for sure but it will also draw pro-Americans from the other parties, including the Democrats as more and more people are concerned for America.

Those who listen to Hannity's show regularly hear him enunciate his Conservative Party affiliation, and he challenges any guest on the show who dares to call him a Republican. Hannity is a little ahead of his time but he can really help as more conservatives choose to leave the Republican Party. Instead of merely joining a state political party for conservatives, they should also become members of the American Party. Hopefully, Sean Hannity will be one of the first to do so.

Though a conservative, just like me—a conservative Democrat, Hannity continues to support Republican conservative candidates. Until recently, Republicans had been and in fact for now, still are the only national party to hold a place for any conservative ideals.

More importantly, for years Republicans had honestly espoused conservative values. Perhaps they have been pretty good fakes over the years but for conservatives, there was no other real game in town. Until the amnesty battle, I thought conservatives and Republicans were on the same side ideologically. Now, I know better.

In mid-August, 2013, Sean Hannity could not hold it back any longer. While I was erupting in this book about not being able to count on supposed avowed conservatives—members of the Republican Party, Hannity also had enough. He saw that the Party of Lincoln had become everything but the Party of Lincoln. So, in mid-August, in a hannitizing moment, on his syndicated radio show, Hannity took the time to discuss Mark Levin's new book, <u>The Liberty Amendments</u>.

I regret that Mr. Levin is not supporting Donald Trump but back then, he was all-in for Republicans and conservatives. Hannity was obviously agitated at the thought that the Republicans were not doing what is necessary to assure the continuous freedom of Americans. Hannity reached crescendo, a place that many conservatives have been waiting to see from many "conservative" political leaders. Hannity pulled no punches on his new disdain for the Republican Party:

"This is it for me. Either they do everything they can do to stop Obamacare– or frankly, in my mind, it's time for a third party. This is now their moment of truth. We're going to learn who the real conservatives are. And we're going to learn who the real establishment people are. And then we're going to have to act accordingly".

It took a while but we now know who the establishment elites are. They run the Party behind the scenes and they are neither conservative nor Republican. They are self-serving big money egotists. They fear Donald Trump because he can end their party with the Republican Party.

Obamacare is just one of many items on the progressive agenda that will hurt everyday Americans. It surely appears that RINO Republicans are ready to cave on all the issues which conservatives hold dear. In late August, 2013, Speaker Boehner advised all House Members to fund Obamacare, a position 100% against the conservative position. I was hoping back then that in 2014, Ohio will shorten Boehner's time as a member of the House, but they reelected him. Eventually, he was forced out of the Speaker's seat.

Republicans, including Speaker John Boehner at the time, instead of being the opposition party were rushing to be as nice to Democrats as they could possibly be. They hoped, perhaps that when Republicans are blown out of existence, or they shoot themselves in the feet, these politicians would be able to gain a sweet spot with the opposition party. They have completely forgotten about the Americans they represent and for a long time have been quite content to leave us in their wake.

Now if only we little conservatives could get the smartest and most eloquent conservative alive, Rush Limbaugh to finally give up the ghost on the GOP, I believe it would cause the floodgates to open and conservatives would be leaving the Republican Party in droves with Chairman Limbaugh's" permission.

Even Rush Limbaugh cannot hold out for long and, though he and Snerdley will not respond to anything I send them, I know that when Rush has had enough of the RINO Republican Party run by the elite establishment, they will rue the day.

We have discussed the name American Party several times in this book. I understand that Sarah Palin also has a great name, "The Freedom Party." As much as I like that name, I also like the name TEA Party. My fear is that Democrats will immediately link Freedom Party to TEA Party.

This would normally be OK. However, through clever deceitful messaging (lies) Democrats have successfully defamed the name *TEA Party*. Consequently, there is a stigma that must be overcome to gain the minds of *dumass* Americans (low information voters).

They already believe that the word *Republican* is bad as well as the term *TEA Party*. It is a very patriotic term and thus, by extension, it would be easy for Democrats to make the *Freedom Party* a synonym for the *TEA Party*. This cannot be done with the name *American Party*. The *American Party* is for Americans.

In many ways, The American Party is not only a great name; it is the best name for any new conservative nationalist party. It is the most innocuous and the most inclusive name for a new Party. What America-loving American cannot like the name *American Party?* Say it with me, please: I am a member of *The American Party!* Doesn't that sound good?

Rush is very smart. He would see that it would work and long before it works, Rush would be a big backer of The American

Party. The Koch Brothers, Paul Ryan, John McCain, Lyndsey Graham, Mitt Romney, Karl Rove, Grover Norquist and a number of big shot elite Republicans will not ever join The American Party. Good!

When Rush Limbaugh joins the American Party and hopefully helps through his wisdom and resources to make the Party successful, he will help our movement more than Obama could ever think of helping the corrupt Democratic Party.

More and more conservatives are mad as hell! Like you and I, they believe that it is time to split the GOP into two separate political parties. I predict that most former GOP will flock to the American Party. Rush Limbaugh, Michael Savage, Sean Hannity, Glenn Beck, Sarah Palin and many others such as Michele Bachman, Michelle Malkin, Mark Steyn, Neil Bortz, Judge Andrew Napolitano, Laura Ingraham (we forgive her for subbing for O'Reilly), and others such as G. Gordon Liddy, seem to be in the on-deck circle of the new show: "The Break-Aways—a story of the flight from the new RINO Republican Party." The Grand Old Party has been AWOL for some time now.

Some elitist spite-mongers that "hate the GOP to be put down though they deserve it," choose to say that the "right wing," of the Republican party, a derogatory term for conservatives, has decided to redefine the term "conservative." They say we should call ourselves the Conservative Party, and get it over with. Though I can appreciate their suggestions; they will not help our cause.

I like saying it so much let me do it again. We should call ourselves *The American Party*, collect our gains and then rule America with Americans who think about America-first. Forget about the liberal progressive Democrats who want to pretend to be for the people. In the backs of their minds, they think of US, as "the proletariat."

The rest of the Republican Party are the "elite establishment." They should win the right to live with the new losing title, *The Republican Party*. We should never let them go ahead and join The American Party to gain any sense of legitimacy for their RINO values.

There are many, many of us who are very saddened and disappointed in what has happened in the Republican Party. I have been a life-long Democrat, who most often voted Republican for conservative reasons. I would have voted for John F. Kennedy if I were old enough, and I did vote for Robert P. Casey Sr., both Democrats because they inspired Americans to be the best that we could be. They did not ask us to quit our jobs and see how great the government would be to us, as our current President suggests.

Though conservatives can make laughing stocks out of the entire Republican Party, it would only be because Republicans have lost their moral compass. Yet, hurting Republicans is not something The American Party is inclined to want to do until we face them in a National Election.

If Republicans were staunch and true, and held on to their sense of the founders' America, neither me, nor any of my conservative friends would be predicting their demise. But, what is; is!

So, I am calling for the elite "establishment" (the Grand Old Party) to check itself out on its new values. This group of RINOS needs to re-unite and redefine the Republican Party as a group of patriots who espouse conservative values. I think that this is all but impossible as their leadership looks upon conservatives as the stubborn, radical, intolerant, staunch religious right, of the far right wing.

The elite Republicans are *fed up* and they resent the spewing of insults and rhetoric toward the GOP. But, conservatives know the rhetoric v turncoat wimpy Republicans is well-deserved. The

GOP "establishment" deserves all the insults. Conservatives are doing a good job of separating the conservative half of the pie from the liberal RINO progressive half, and the GOP, like it or not is divided, though perhaps not enough.

Conservatives hate this type of negative speech coming from the left, but it is really disgusting when it comes from the elite in the Republican Party.

Conservatives are not looking to be rabble rousers in the Republican Party but we are treated like dirt, nonetheless. We do ask questions about the fervor of the Republicans to execute on the values that they espouse publically. We do worry that they are about to pull the rug out from conservatism at any moment. Whoever would have thought many elitist Republicans such as Meg Whitman, and the three Bush gentlemen would openly support Hillary Clinton over Donald Trump. Even I did not see that one coming.

Some suggest that the larger question is whether Republicans have the courage to fight for the principles of individual freedom and opportunity that built the prosperity that Democrats seek to exploit for their ideological purposes. There would be no talk about a new American Party of conservatives if we thought Republicans were up to the task, and if we thought Republicans would embrace long-time American values.

The American Party is for Americans!

The American Party, as proposed in this book certainly has a much better ring to it than "Know Nothing," the one-time pseudonym for the party in the mid 1800's. Moreover, the term "American Party" should be able to attract not only disenfranchised conservative Republicans but also those Democrats, Greens, Libertarians, and Constitutionals who hold strong conservative views.

The name "American Party is not new but the idea is new in that this is to be the rallying point for conservatives in all other parties, not just Republicans . The political party name of American Party has been around several times in the US over the years. Here are just some of the instances:

- The Toleration party of Connecticut was also known as the American Party. It was established to oppose the Federalist Party.
- The partisan name American Party was used by the Know-Nothing movement based on nativism and existed in 1855-56.
- In Utah, the American Party existed from 1905 to 1911. Its purpose was to challenge the Mormons.
- The American Party of Nebraska ran Mary Kennery (or Kennedy) as a favorite daughter for President of the United States in 1952.
- In 1969, the American Party succeeded the 1968 American Independent Party.
- In 1968, the American Independent Party put George Wallace on the ballot for President.

Some of the uses of the name as shown above are not in synch with our idea of a party of Americans for America. There are other derivatives of the American Party which deserve note as the same notion of patriotism for the good of America was their overriding theme. Perhaps you can recall the America First Party from 2002; the American Conservative Party from 2008; and the American Freedom Party from 2010.

Last on the list of similar names is America's Party, which was formed under a different name as a conservative American political party. It was formed in August 2008 by supporters of Alan Keyes as an alternative to the Republican, Democratic and other parties. Too bad these parties did not make it. The one and only American Party, a splinter group originating from the

Republican Party after the 2016 elections and embracing conservatives from all other parties can make it for sure.

The new "American Party" will replace the outmoded and cowardly Republican Party. In the residual Republican Party, the ghost of Burt Lahr should be cast to play the part of the Republican Party when the move is finally made. He would make a great cowardly lion!

The American Party is necessary as a party to embrace real Americans. Conservatives, such as those that are being disrespected and expelled from the Republican Party, as I speak will become the backbone of this patriotic American party.

Conservatives are happy to permit both Republicans and Democrats to swim in their own brine of corruption. They have chosen a path that does help them but does not help regular Americans. Let's hope all good dedicated Americans from every Party join the American Party in droves as it forms and as it embraces the values of conservatism.

Chapter 15   The American Party in 2020!

Sarah Palin was a victim of GOP RINOS

Before I go on recognizing Sarah Palin for her good works and I talk about her in a very positive light to help make my case on the American Party, let me clarify a few things that may have gotten lost for those who use the corrupt press to get their news.

Like the American people, Sarah Palin is simply another victim of Obama lies and perpetrations and by a Republican Party too wimpy to defend its own candidate. No wonder Donald Trump cherishes the endorsement of this tough lady and fine American patriot. As time moved by from 2008, we saw even Palin bashing everywhere from Saturday Night Live to Katie Couric, to anything supporting the Democratic Party. They shoot to kill.

They are shooting again. This time metaphorically in 2016 Donald Trump gets to play the role of Sarah Palin as the same corrupt press that did its best to destroyed Palin is well on its scurrilous path to take out Donald Trump "for the good of America." Hah!

The American people who pay any attention to the truth, realize the lies behind the various narratives from the Obama administration, their elected and appointed progressive/liberal government officials, always obligingly delivered by a complicit, corrupt mainstream media. As time goes by, will anybody be able to trust NBC, CBS, MSNBC CBS, ABC, or even The New

York Times. Both the political left and the media will lose credibility, support and relevance as real Americans step up to the plate and say, "Enough!"

God bless Sarah Palin for her fortitude and overall moxie in dealing with the pigs in the media. Mike Nieman from the Baltimore Sun wrote that "She withstood the onslaught from the left with dignity and poise, not getting down to their level as they savaged her with ridicule and name calling straight from Saul Alinsky's book "Rules for Radicals." Personal attack was the only weapon the left could use against her because they could not go against her sterling record in Alaska and near 90 percent approval among Alaskans. Sarah will be vindicated and the left discredited as the truth emerges."

Andrew James Breitbart took a liking to the true Palin story. Breitbart as many know was an American conservative publisher, commentator for The Washington Times, journalist, author, and television and radio personality on various news programs, who served as an editor for the Drudge Report website. His work persists and is continued at www.breitbart.com. He uncovered a lot of nasty political dirt in his day and when he died of "natural causes on March 2012, at just 43 years of age, many felt that foul play was involved.

Andrew Breitbart once said: "Sarah Palin has been inundated with the greatest assault known to humankind against a pure innocent." He had a big problem with how Palin was treated. He produced the film "Undefeated" to help right the record:

"I'm attacking the Republican establishment, so I'm saying this isn't about the Democratic Party," he said. "This is about the Republican establishment that watched her maligned and eviscerated by the very forces that they go to great lengths to placate because they know it could happen to them to. And so the lack of chivalry from the male Caucasian establishment while she's being kicked mercilessly was a very important lesson for me to learn about how politics is done in Washington."

"I want Sarah Palin to get in there to join Thaddeus McCotter and Michele Bachmann and Herman Cain and any number of anti-establishment, anti-Beltway candidates, and I want them to fight it out 'Apprentice'-style, 'Survivor'-style, 'American Idol'-style," he said.

Breitbart did a great film on Sarah Palin after meeting her just three times simply because he could not stand the inhuman treatment she received from the corrupt press. He said: "In two quick hours, people will have not just their opinion of Sarah Palin reset, but it serves to show just how predictably evil the mainstream media can behave."

Stephen K. Bannon's powerful documentary, "The Undefeated," may very well have been intended to be the condensed story of Sarah Palin to date. However, it is much more than that. "The Undefeated" is America's story and it is a story of American Exceptionalism. Likewise it is the story of all of us if we consider ourselves to be genuine Reagan Conservatives.

The story primarily is about Conservatives, Tea Party types and GOP primary voters. Bannon gets right to the massive force and tension that came from the confrontation of what the author views as Palin pitted against elitist, establishment forces intent on, not simply opposing, but destroying both Palin and the entire world of the conservatives—what she represents.

If you are not impressed with Sarah Palin and what a fighter she has always been, read more about her and you will be. The irony in 2016 is that in many ways such a film would depict the evil media again but this time working on the credibility of Donald Trump. Again, this time, the Republican establishment elites are piling on, and not defending their candidate. How strange?

Sarah Palin is a conservative hero. I thank the Lord for such people with such guts! Sarah Palin will not only like the American Party, she will be one of its most cherished leaders.

There is no question about that regardless of how small the diminutive Katie Couric tries to make her. Palin stands tall among all women and among all men. Democrats fear her because they know that regular people, especially women, would quickly fall in love with her courage and her patriotism. We would be so lucky to have her in a national office of prominence.

Ronald Reagan is a long-time conservative hero and he was supported by the GOP at a time when the Left tried to make a mockery of him as a potential leader, and then again as he led America to greatness. Reagan goes down in history as a loving father, a devoted husband, and a fine human being. Like many of us, he had issues with some of his children but like US, he loved them regardless and he surely still does in heaven.

Many of us know that Ronald Reagan once famously said: "I didn't leave the Democrat Party, the Democrat Party left me." These days, millions of conservatives around the country feel the same about a Republican Party seemingly hell-bent on abandoning every conservative principle other than crony capitalism. When we leave the Republican Party en masse, conservatives, just like Reagan will say: "We didn't leave the Republican Party, the Republican Party left US."

Several years ago, one of our conservative rock stars, Sarah Palin let out some frustration when she offered to leave the Republican Party to form the Freedom party. Palin said:

"I love the name of that party – 'Freedom Party.' And if the GOP continues to back away from the planks in our platform, from the principles that built this party of Lincoln and Reagan, then yeah, more and more of us are going to start saying, 'You know, what's wrong with being independent,' kind of with that libertarian streak that much of us have. In other words, we want government to back off and not infringe upon our rights. I think there will be a lot of us who start saying 'GOP, if you abandon us, we have nowhere else to go except to become more independent and not enlisted in a one or the other private majority parties that rule in our nation, either a Democrat or a

Republican.' Remember these are private parties, and you know, no one forces us to be enlisted in either party."

I think that if you substitute the words American Party for Freedom Party, rock star Sarah Palin would still concur with her message above.

Like many of us, Sarah Palin would prefer to get the GOP to change rather than have to break completely away. She thinks that it would not be a good thing for conservatives to start over to create a third party movement that she feels would take decades to realize. On this point, the rock star and I disagree. I see the American Party as the magnet that will pull 60 to 70% of Americans together almost immediately. Americans are waiting to join the American Party but it does not exist yet.

Mrs Palin thinks the solution to the Republican Party should come from within since we have lost too much freedom, liberty, and morality. She thinks that to capture it back with a third party movement would take too long without having the big umbrella of the Republican Party. She thinks it would take decades but at the same time she worries that it won't be too long before America disappears if the Republicans continue to be led by the RINOS.

If the organization of The American Party is done in a half-baked manner then she is right. It will take decades. But, if all the big conservative names (not the Republican or RINO names) form an organization to professionally handle the formation of the Party, and if it is extremely well funded, and if it were begun reasonably soon, it could be ready to go in the 2020 Presidential Election. With no TV, no radio, and no cell phones, and no Internet, it took just a little less than two years for the original Republican Party to get the organization job done. With the major advances in communications today; the job can be done even sooner.

At the US History site,
http://www.ushistory.org/gop/origins.htm, in the GOP section,
the editors put together a very brief piece showing the events of
the days back when that led to the formation of the Republican
Party. Their opening one liner describes perfectly the rationale
for a new party both then and now:

"Trying times spawn new forces."

Their first full paragraph sums up the trying times of those times
quite nicely:

*"The Missouri Compromise of 1820 divided the country at
the36° 30' parallel between the pro-slavery, agrarian South
and anti-slavery, industrial North, creating an uneasy peace
which lasted for three decades. This peace was shattered in
1854 by the Kansas-Nebraska Act. Settlers would decide if
their state would be free or slave. Northern leaders such as
Horace Greeley, Salmon Chase and Charles Sumner could
not sit back and watch the flood of pro-slavery settlers cross
the parallel. A new party was needed."*

These are different times but trying times nonetheless. An
abridged timeline is also given on the history site and is shown in
the next two paragraphs:

*"Where was the party born? Following the publication of the
"Appeal of Independent Democrats" in major newspapers,
spontaneous demonstrations occurred. In early 1854, the first
proto-Republican Party meeting took place in Ripon,
Wisconsin. On June 6, 1854 on the outskirts of Jackson,
Michigan upwards of 10,000 people turned out for a mass
meeting "Under the Oaks." This led to the first organizing
convention in Pittsburgh on February 22, 1856.*

*"The gavel fell to open the Party's first nominating convention,
in Philadelphia, Pennsylvania, on June 17, 1856, announcing
the birth of the Republican Party as a unified political force."*

Sarah Palin's worst nightmare has the conservatives leaving the "comforts of the Republican Party." She fears that it would mean that every election consequence would go to the Democrats for the next several decades and leave conservatives meaningless in the political landscape for America. As much as I like Mrs. Palin, I think she need not have such deep fears and nightmares.

Just like the original Republican Party, which was able to form in two years, which lost with Fremont, and then won with Lincoln four years later, the American Party can get the job done even quicker. Not only that but with all of our modern methods of communication, we can surely be ready by 2020 with a candidate that can actually win the presidency such as Donald Trump in his second term. Perhaps after that it might be Sarah Palin herself, or Mike Lee or Ted Cruz or perhaps the inimitable Dr. Benjamin Carson. The American Party is ready to be brought to life right now!

Though Palin would love to lead an exodus, she is at best ambivalent about the probability of success. She likes to think that the idea of bailing on the GOP is a great idea but then her practical side says that it is not feasible. She cites that the two most viable right-of-center 3rd Parties -- the Libertarian and Constitution Parties -- still have not been able to achieve ballot access in all 50 states, and she acknowledges the importance of ballot access to the success of her notion of a "Freedom Party."

She is partially correct, but here is where the American Party is different from the Libertarians, Greens, or Constitutionals. The number of conservatives in the country teaming up with the pro-Americans in an American Party would be huge. No Party since the Republicans left the Whigs did a huge chunk of a Party get excised by any Party in its initial organization. The American Party is win-win-win. The Party wins, conservatives win, and the American people win.

Having a name that is cuddly and loving such as The American Party will help more than a name like the Freedom Party, which can be quickly morphed by conservative-hating Democrats into the TEA Party.

Ironically, the secret name of the "Know Nothing Party," leading up to the formation of the Republican Party was The American Party. How appropriate now that the American Party be brought back to win the day from Republicans.

No matter how much it might help to be able to take over the Republican Party with conservative thought, the fact is the Party is broken as a bastion for conservatives. Unfortunately, we are all here, right now, in this book, because the Republicans have let us down. We are ready to form the American Party as a solution to combat RINO Republicanism, which has no plans to go away any time soon. Our only hope is that the RINO elitist establishment quickly join with the Democrats. They will be easy defeated when they join the donkeys.

As a Democrat, I know I would be attracted to the American Party. All of those negative big business notions that come with the word "Republican," would disappear. In addition to at least 80% of the members of the Republican Party, small time Democrats, like in my home town, who do not adhere to the views of regular hard-line Party leaders, would leave the Democrat Party in droves to join the American Party.

I can see this Party in just a few years bringing in 2/3 of the population to each election. Long live America and the American Party! Of course, the Democrats would naturally become the anti-American Party, which they are now already, without the nomenclature.

Chapter 16   Obama and Fascism— Love and Marriage

Even in Italy, they call it Fascism

To make sure as we discuss fascism and Obama that we are talking about the same thing; let us take a look at the Random House Dictionary definition. Fascism is "a governmental system led by a dictator having complete power, forcibly suppressing opposition and criticism, regimenting all industry, commerce, etc., and emphasizing an aggressive nationalism and often racism."

With the takeover of healthcare, the auto industry, and the tight control over pipelines and oil reserves on government lands, Obama, one industry at a time has been taking over US industry and commerce while Congress remains motionless. Has the Republican opposition gone on permanent vacation? I am so glad Trump is pro-American.

As we break down the definition of Fascism into component phrases, we find that we also have created a definition for the era of Obama. Look at his "accomplishments" since taking office in 2009: It frightens the soul to see what this man has done and what he is doing to America. He has become a dictator in chief and he laughs at Congress and the Constitution as he does his own thing.

For eight years Republicans have been afraid even to mention possible impeachment as a solution for this rogue president but his lawlessness is worthy of losing his office and being tried for high crimes and misdemeanors. Republicans have not only abandoned conservatives; they have abandoned their own self-worth as they sit and cower in Congress hoping they do not upset this de-facto dictator.

Obama has become the master of the Executive Order but his orders often have no basis in law. He operates outside the US Constitution. The President has even abandoned the notion of due process and habeas corpus for those branded by the President as "enemy combatants." There is a rebarbative expansion of the secret surveillance state, and of course the President has assumed tacit control over some of the largest segments of industry including those already mentioned. Yes, even in Italy, they call this Fascism.

Besides heavy manufacturing and the oil industry, look at his impact on banks, insurance, and of course health care. Are we better off having this incompetent dictator in charge of our lives? Of course not, yet the Republicans again stand silent as Obama destroys America. What business has he ever run? Thank you for your quiet, no sound response. I agree. A man with no business experience by osmosis is now the Businessperson in Chief. His heir apparent, Hillary Clinton is similarly devoid of business experience.

Under various versions of Fascism, what would be a formerly a free society, such as the United States, gets divided into various segments that have a purpose in fascism. For example, black, white, workers, managers, young, old, etc. take on meaning based on what they represent. These several notions are then bound together by governmental control. Left on their own in the scenario regulated by Fascism, these various factions would destroy one another and cause their own mutual destruction. But first they must help the dictator.

Did we all not see in the 2012 Democratic Convention an attempt to classify people by their beliefs, their religion, their sex, their sexual orientation, their race or national origin, and their legal status? Mussolini could not think of all the ways to divide the Italians or Fascism may have worked for him.

Thanks to the benevolent bureaucracy provided by pure Fascism, all partisans are kept peacefully in check and nobody is permitted to kill or hurt anybody else. Thus the state gains as the people learn that they have no rights and the sooner they learn that they are nothing compared to the state, the sooner they can contribute to the stability and growth of the state.

Of course it will not take long for regular people who do not want to go along with the prescriptions meted out by the state, to do so anyway or face punishments. In Fascism, the people fear that the axe inevitably will fall, and life will no longer be good. The axe may even kill them or their families if they interfere. And, when they do not go along with the state, they find that maxim to be 100% true. Take another look at Obama and also please look at Hillary, his anointed successor. Why is it that the Republican Party is not telling you what I just did?

Anybody who works against the unity of the Fascist state will know the meaning of the axe, and will know it is not folklore. In 2016 of course, in the US, the axe is really a symbol and it represents some level of social marginalization that would naturally be followed by a form of economic enslavement.

Who among us, especially the millennials, can honestly say life is great and their productivity is needed for the country to survive. Let's just use the fall of 2016 as an example. Who will be the first to say how good things are. There are now 90,000,000+ Americans who have dropped out of the work force. Over ten million of these made the decision after their UC benefits expired.

Millennials have the opposite problem. They can't get into the workplace and if they did and then got laid off, they would be an unfortunate statistic in the UC ratings and the rate, well managed by Democrats might go up and the party would suffer. So, in many ways it is better for millennials to be denied their first job for they would have too many years to mess up the Obama labor statistics.

Just like Hitler's Youth, back when the Fuhrer was controlling all things in Germany via Executive Order, millennials have been duped but Hitler left no doubt in the minds he controlled. Obama's youth may very well recant if their cell phone batteries from their free phones are not replaced regularly by the government.

If you are a millennial today, you have been duped. Know it or not, you have had the greatest sin perpetrated against you. Your future has been stolen by an egotistic narcissist who thinks all things should be measured in the way things affect him. You do not matter but for him. You will soon learn how to survive in a Fascist state—if nothing changes from the big change you voted into office.

Some suggest that in the IRS spying world, the NSA spying world, the Benghazi lying world, and the notion that the President would lie when he is spying on his enemies, that Americans are worse off than when their nasty neighbors in the 1700's would accuse them of being for or against the Crown. Do you think that it is possible that in our lifetime, the big black cars will be pulling into our neighborhoods taking people, your parents probably, away to the gulags—never to be seen again? Could that happen in the USA?

In today's America, the potentially politically ostracized can be easily watched by cameras everywhere, linked together by sophisticated software. The frightening part of course is that the cameras are owned by the federal domestic spying apparatus, controlled by Barack Hussein Obama.

But, Americans are told not to worry since the warrantless wiretaps that are in place to listen and to record the electronic communications of all Americans, are needed to solve the problem we have with terrorists.

Ironically, just a few years earlier the regime now in charge of surveillance, suggested these terrorists were not to be feared and their acts should not be castigated as terrorist. Instead, as US forces approached their forces, instead of thinking we were fighting a global war on terror, the new rhetoric pointed to something liberal progressives like to call "overseas contingency operations." There were no terrorists. Perhaps the government is the new terrorist? Has the Republican Party sufficiently explained this phenomenon to the America people? Where have they been?

Does it matter if the President is a socialist, a communist, a liberal or a progressive?

Recent polls have shown that as many as 55% of Americans believe that Barack Obama is a "socialist." Many Americans believe that Obama is leading the nation on a "road to socialism." Hillary Clinton would ask us what difference it makes and most thinking Americans would reply that it matters because America Matters! How would you respond?

Even Democrats, when challenged for the truth would tell US all that America has, over the years, had inclinations towards being socialist, even a fascist nation in many ways for many decades, especially since FDR's New Deal. From Wilson forward, Americans had to check communism at the gate. Until now, however it was relatively easy. The President was never known to be a communist in those past days. Is Obama for America or simply for Obama winning every game he plays? Is he a Fascist or a Communist? What is Hillary as taught by Saul Alinsky?

Ironically, no President before Obama threw it in our face and blamed his socialism for the economic malaise from which the country could not recover. Perhaps if the President took a three month or six month vacation, the economy could fix itself. But, with his business crippling regulations, it will not happen on its own. Thankfully there is a Donald Trump on the horizon.

We have discussed Fascism so far in this chapter and the President's implementation. Yet, it would still help if we all understood socialism / fascism because progressive liberals are on either and / or both of these two sides.

What is socialism v. fascism?

Many theorists, including Mussolini himself, have slotted Fascism as completely opposite socialism. In fact, the principles of Fascism are very hostile to what are called liberal democracies, socialism, and communism. All fascist undertakings share certain common features. These include the primacy of the state as well as the veneration of the state, a devotion to a strong leader, a heavy emphasis on nationalism and militarism. Does any of this seem familiar? How about "devotion to a strong leader," competent or incompetent!

Fascists see political violence, war, and imperialism as necessary to rejuvenate the nation. Proponents of fascism are not embarrassed by becoming powerful. In fact, they believe intrinsically that stronger nations have the absolute right to obtain land and resources by warring with weaker nations and displacing them from their wealth. In essence fascism subjugates the individual and the notion of the public in favor of the state. The supremacy of the state should need no further explanation. The individual and the groups simply do not matter.

The Ayn Rand Lexicon (aynrandlexicon.com) makes the contrast in very clear language as follows: "The main characteristic of socialism (and of communism) is public ownership of the means of production, and, therefore, the abolition of private property. The right to property is the right of use and disposal. Under fascism, men retain the semblance or pretense of private property, but the government holds total power over its use and disposal."

Socialism is often equated with fascism, and though in practice in countries that have adopted one or the other philosophies, there is often a mix of fascism and socialism. Yet, in such states, socialism has some substantially different properties from fascism. The main tenet of socialism as dictated from Marxian principles is the public ownership of wealth, property and the means of production. So, of course Obama is also a socialist.

Chapter 17   Obama: Wilson, Bulworth, Roosevelt?

Socialism is the Obama ticket

The President expressed being a socialist for the first time in mid May 2013 after keeping it in for his whole first term. Obama in fact told the NY Times that he was thinking about "Going Bulworth," and all that brings with it.

In other words, Obama admitted being a closet socialist who would love to come out of the closet. Bulworth of course, as movie goers know, was a main character—Senator Jay Bulworth, a closet socialist, played by Warren Beatty in the 1998 hit movie titled, "Bulworth."

Woodrow Wilson did more for socialism than any other president by enabling the notion of redistribution of wealth. The Personal Income Tax brought in under the Wilson regime was the source of funding that took the earnings of hard working Americans and gave them to those who had not earned the wages. This today is known as redistribution of income. Americans have always been chumps for a sob story.

Wilson's adoption of the Personal Income Tax gave all Presidents from that point in history the opportunity to use the public's money for social engineering endeavors. All such schemes are against the Constitution but this did not matter to Wilson, Franklin Roosevelt, Lyndon Johnson, or Obama. With lots of revenue from the new taxes, Wilson was able to achieve his goal of using "practical means of realizing for society the principles of socialism" by unshackling state power.

Wilson had a radical political science agenda but was unable to achieve all of his socialist objectives in two terms but he did a lot of damage nonetheless. His revitalized democratic political science notions addressed the issues he identified. Wilson had a "different" view of policy, organization, and administration and he brought this view to his actions through his long career in the academy and in politics.

Having eradicated the significance of individual rights for democracy in his writings, Wilson went on to decree that the Constitution was not the final word. He was not a fan of the Constitution and he strongly advocated eliminating the separation of powers. From his perspective, just like Obama ruling by Executive Orders, Wilson hoped it would unleash unlimited majority party government for the Democrats. Wilson, though a Democrat believed he could bring practicality to the demands of socialism, and he openly suggested that socialism should be the ruling ideology of his Party.

Thankfully, America is structured to survive people like Woodrow Wilson, and Barack H. Obama, and their innate desire to crush America, the land of the free. Wilson would have done well as President of the USSR. Over time, poor leaders such as Wilson and Barack Hussein Obama are apt to appear, hoping to take all Americans down a trail that the founders never imagined. We can prevent another such leader from taking control of America by saying "NO" to Hillary in 2016.

Obama and Roosevelt

Having both chambers of Congress in control of Republicans right now should be enough to be a powerful countervailing power against this potentially terminal disease for America. But, Republicans have chosen to lie down with Democrats rather than oppose them. The good ness of countervailing power cannot be achieved if Republicans continue to be wimps and choose to provide no pushback and they keep the public uninformed with no solid information about what is really happening behind the scenes in Washington.

Wilson was not the last Democrat who used social engineering to push a socialist agenda. Franklin D. Roosevelt is credited by many of our parents and parents' parents with saving America from the depression. The fact is that Roosevelt's policies lengthened the depression.

There was no communication back then, other than radio that could have helped our parents to know the truth. There were no talk shows, just the sanitized news every hour for a few minutes. And, so many of US, until we really check out FDR, think he was a great economic hero.

He was a great hero, but not in economics. The only person he knew more about on economic matters had yet to be born – Barack H. Obama. And, so now, we are stuck with the new Roosevelt who could not tie Roosevelt's shoes on economic matters. Ironically, Roosevelt could not tie his own shoes on economic matters.

Like Roosevelt, however, Obama is ostensibly committed to greater equality and he will go through great lengths to achieve it. Who cares who must pay for government mistakes to achieve the nirvana of full equality?

Back in 1943 for example when Roosevelt was looking to pay for the war, he faced lawmakers who, like today, were opposed to taxing just the rich. Roosevelt found a way to do it that made him appear like the dictator that Obama has become. Check out the similarities in style of a past President who also thought Congress did not matter.

Roosevelt's deal was called the New Deal and it was a back room deal for sure. It may have helped somewhat in helping some people in the country recover, nobody really knows for sure.

Roosevelt used the shotgun approach to taxation. Every potential tax source was taxed and taxed heavily. Roosevelt used regressive and progressive taxation to grab bucks for the treasury from wherever he saw a buck. Most Americans excuse him as he was "trying to finance the war," but Roosevelt, like Obama believed he had some special gift that enabled him to bypass the people and the Congress (representatives of the people) to supposedly serve the people.

His most important source of New Deal revenue was excise taxes levied on alcoholic beverages, cigarettes, matches, candy, chewing gum, margarine, fruit juice, soft drinks, cars, tires (including even the tires on wheelchairs), telephone calls, movie tickets, playing cards, electricity, radios. To get the revenue from alcohol, he did repeal prohibition. There were many other everyday things subject to New Deal excise taxes. The bottom line is that the progressive FDR brought forth the most regressive taxes and many of them.

The New Deal was paid for by the middle class and poor people. They blamed the government not Roosevelt. It surely is ironic that even to hear one of FDR's famous "Fireside Chats," taxpayers had to pay FDR an excise tax for having a radio and using electricity!

FDR's demands were quite excessive by anyone's standards. For example, he also proposed a 100 percent top personal tax rate. Sounds fair to me—hah! Think about the incentive to get you up in the morning and go to work for no pay. Roosevelt took Wilson's corporate and personal income tax to the nth degree to grab revenue for the government and he found other sources to keep the treasury close to being in the black. Of course, Obama Red is the Treasury's new color. Despite all of Roosevelt's income sources, the economy got worse. Entrepreneur's figured, "Why work?"

Roosevelt taxed everything that he could find and even things like services which were invisible. Roosevelt's message to Congress was that at a time of "grave national danger, no American citizen ought to have a net income, after he has paid his taxes, of more than $25,000 a year."

Conservative lawmakers rejected FDR's plan before the ink was dry. Obsessed with desiring more earnings to tax, in a few months, Roosevelt tried again. Again Congress blew him off.

Like the Obama man with nine lives, the same Obama who came back to life and survived Sarah Palin's convention speech, FDR would not back down. He was back a month later but this time, he pulled an Obama. By Executive order, Roosevelt single handedly limited top corporate salaries to $25,000 after taxes. So, although Obama is bad and is socialist, he did not invent the tyranny which he practices. He had some great mentors, such as Roosevelt and Wilson. Obama is preparing to be Hillary Clinton's mentor as he is planning to live in Washington DC in 2017.

Back when members of Academia were not all progressives, Princeton economist Harley Lutz along with enraged conservatives found their blood boiling. Lutz said: "the only logical stopping place for this movement, would be a completely communistic equalization of incomes."

Back in the 1940's Republicans were not wanna-be Democrats and rather than accept Obamacare as our gutless Republicans have done, they vowed to kill FDR's executive order to tax the rich into oblivion by any legislative means necessary. As soon as they could, they attached a rider repealing his order to a bill that would give the wartime debt ceiling a desperately needed lift. FDR tried but failed to get that rider thrown out. The bill became law without his signature. He had no choice.

That is the predicament that strong Republicans must use to stop Obama. He must have no choice. Despite winning this victory, Roosevelt was determined to sap the wealth from America's richest taxpayers. By the end of the war, America's most wealthy would be paying taxes on income over $200,000 at a 94 percent statutory rate. Yet, even that was not 100% as Roosevelt had intended.

Please do not share these percentages with Obama or Hillary Clinton!

Thank you.

Chapter 18 The American Party & Elbert Lee Guillory Give Conservative Americans Hope

Hope Springs Eternal

Intrinsically each and every conservative knows what conservatism is. In a nutshell it is for things that are good and it includes a sharp rejection for things that are bad. More technically, conservatism can be defined as a political or theological orientation advocating the preservation of the best in society and opposing radical changes.

It is clearly a puzzlement that the Republican Party has begun, piece by piece to replace its conservative foundation with the godless notion that the ends justify the means, and the only end for the Republican establishment today is to win elections. The people on the other hand see no value in a victory that provides the poor values of the Democratic Party. Why bother?

In his work, An Essay on Man, Alexander Pope offers consolation to those who continue to hope that something good will happen although it seems unlikely. In many ways, this fits the hopelessness that conservatives find today in the Republican Party, and for other reasons, across all of America.

Hope springs eternal in the human breast;
Man never is, but always to be blessed:
The soul, uneasy and confined from home,
Rests and expatiates in a life to come.

There are a number of interpretations of this classic poem but all have the same overall meaning. In the original poem shown above, Pope makes the argument that God did not give any of us knowledge of our future for it would be too heavy for us to bear. Instead, he gave us, in our ignorance, hope and optimism that the future will be good.

And, so, people throughout history continue to hope even though they have evidence that things more than likely will not turn out the way they want. We conservatives can use this as a rallying cry for the Republican Party, hoping it will change in a miraculous way.

As an alternate thought, as we have discussed in this book from Chapter One, there is always the hope that the American Party will take the place of the Republican Party in our hearts and that it will become a huge success for the nation. Hope Springs Eternal is often said during times of hardship and is meant to encourage people to keep hope alive.

Let us keep our hope alive in one of the two positive outcomes as defined. However, we do not have all day to decide which path to follow.

I am seeing small snippets of hope as hard core liberal progressives and the corrupt media seem to be softening a small bit. There is no longer the absolute fear in offending Obama or Hillary or any other liberal progressive icon. Even liberal radio personnel are seeing things differently and Rush Limbaugh, the eternal optimist is not only doing his normal conservative cheerleading, he is delving into the complicated reasons why people at one time felt so good about President Obama.

More than anything, the fact that the president's polling numbers have come down from excessive highs like hot bricks is more than enough reason to have hope. Hope Springs Eternal that the American People, including progressive liberals will see the light and follow that path that God would want.

Ironically, as Democrats may be seeing a spark of light, I see Republicans beginning to hold on to Democratic values and Democratic notions instead of doing what they can to stop the threat brought forth by Democrat principles and the lack thereof.

Conservatives had been counting on Republicans to help America for years. It seemed natural. Since the Republican leadership has turned its back on conservatives, I have been compelled to write this book to help conservatives have hope and a very good alternative to the new Republican way. Hope may spring eternal that Republicans will see the light but as in the poem, it is not likely.

And so, we must create our own hope by knowing that we can build the American Party as a better replacement for the Republican Party than the one time Party of Lincoln ever hoped to be. We can begin as the Party of Trump in his second term (2020). When the American Party blooms, we will all gain from fallout from Republicans, Democrats, Libertarians, Constitutionals, and Greens. There is even hope that Independents will find the American Party suiting their ideals and a number may choose to join the Party to help it along.

Elbert Lee Guillory

Hope comes from many sources. One of the greatest moments of hope for the country came forth just a few years ago as Louisiana State Senator Elbert Guillory (R-Opelousas) switched from the Democrat Party to the Republican Party. In his essay, he explains in detail why he made the decision to switch. Along the way, he talks about the history of the Republican Party, from when it was founded as an abolitionist movement in 1854. The Senator then talks about how the welfare state is only a mechanism for politicians to control the black community. His essay is very compelling and it is presented in its entirety below

Since Elbert Guillory is a black man, his perspectives are quite salient. Unfortunately, like all black conservatives, Guillory will soon find himself being impugned and besmirched by his former party as if he has somehow gone mad. Dr. Ben Carson, the surgeon from John Hopkins who spoke at the National Prayer Breakfast, and then ran as a Presidential hopeful in the 2016 Republican Primary is an example of what will happen to the Senator. Carson is already being called 'token,' 'Uncle Tom,' 'Oreo,' and of course "Nigger." Carson is not about to cave to such attacks and I have a good feeling about Guillory. Here is the essay he wrote about why he switched parties. It will make a good conservative melt and be recharged with hope.

"

Hello, my name is Elbert Lee Guillory, and I'm the senator for the twenty-fourth district right here in beautiful Louisiana. Recently I made what many are referring to as a bold decision to switch my party affiliation to the Republican Party. I wanted to take a moment to explain why I became a Republican, and also to explain why I don't think it was a bold decision at all. It is the right decision not only for me but for all my brothers and sisters in the black community.

You see, in recent history the Democrat Party has created the illusion that their agenda and their policies are what's best for black people. Somehow it has been forgotten that the Republican Party was founded in 1854 as an abolitionist movement with one simple creed: that slavery is a violation of the rights of man.

Frederick Douglass called Republicans the Party of freedom and progress, and the first Republican president was Abraham Lincoln, the author of the Emancipation Proclamation. It was the Republicans in Congress who authored the thirteenth, fourteenth, and fifteenth amendments giving former slaves citizenship, voting rights, and due process of law.

The Democrats on the other hand were the Party of Jim Crow. It was Democrats who defended the rights of slave owners. It was the Republican President Dwight Eisenhower who championed the Civil Rights Act of 1957, but it was Democrats in the Senate who filibustered the bill.

You see, at the heart of liberalism is the idea that only a great and powerful big government can be the benefactor of social justice for all Americans. But the left is only concerned with one thing—control. And they disguise this control as charity. Programs such as welfare, food stamps—these programs aren't designed to lift black Americans out of poverty, they were always intended as a mechanism for politicians to control the black community.

The idea that blacks, or anyone for that matter, need the government to get ahead in life is despicable. And even more important, this idea is a failure. Our communities are just as poor as they've always been. Our schools continue to fail children. Our prisons are filled with young black men who should be at home being fathers. Our self-initiative and our self-reliance have been sacrificed in exchange for allegiance to our overseers who control us by making us dependent on them.

Sometimes I wonder if the word freedom is tossed around so frequently in our society that it has become a cliché.

The idea of freedom is complex and it is all-encompassing. It's the idea that the economy must remain free of government persuasion. It's the idea that the press must operate without government intrusion. And it's the idea that the emails and phone records of Americans should remain free from government search and seizure. It's the idea that parents must be the decision makers in regards to their children's education not some government bureaucrat.

But most importantly, it is the idea that the individual must be free to pursue his or her own happiness free from government dependence and free from government control. Because to be truly free is to be reliant on no one other than the author of our destiny. These are the ideas at the core of the Republican Party, and it is why I am a Republican.

So my brothers and sisters of the American community, please join with me today in abandoning the government plantation and the Party of disappointment. So that we may all echo the words of one Republican leader who famously said, free at last, free at last, thank God Almighty, we are free at last..."

-- End of Guillory remarks –

Yes, the Republican Party is a much better choice than the Democrat Party, even though it is not holding 100% true to its values.

The American Party will take all of those values and add even more to help Americans be successful and to help Americans remain free for all time.

Chapter 19   The American Party & Dr. Ben Carson—Hope 4 Americans

Pediatric Neurosurgeon would be a great president

It is so infrequently that something really; really, good happens on the conservative side. I mean something good enough that it may save America. Though most of this book points out the hopeless nature of our predicament with weak Republican legislators, I feel good about the possibility of something good coming as I write this chapter.

At least now I understand why liberal progressives have been so excited about Barack Obama that they made him their personal president. I do admit that when he first came on the scene three years ago, I had similar emotions about Dr. Ben Carson. At the time, Dr. Carson was Head of Pediatric Neurosurgery at Johns Hopkins Hospital in Baltimore, Md. Of course he is the same Dr. Carson who impressed us all at the Presidential Debates in the Spring 2016.

After hearing his speech at the National Prayer Breakfast, February 7, 2013, I was very encouraged that people such as Dr. Carson actually still exist in America. You don't have to be a brain surgeon to see a world of difference between the real Barack Obama and the real Ben Carson. The real Ben Carson supports Donald Trump for president and the real Barack Obama supports Hillary Clinton.

Though Obama led a preferred life having gone to the best schools, and having been reared in a household where there was no shortage of money. Carson led a tough life and was reared by a single mom who disciplined her children more than most, and lived in a home that was made nice by mom but which had a lot of things missing. There was no money to buy many of the finer things in life.

Obama's credentials include a lot of resume puffery; never had a real job; had a hard time relating to regular Americans—both black and white, and his best work in life was as a community organizer, a position that folks like me, who grew up poor and did not know it, had never heard about until Obama ran for President.

Our President is undeniably one of the worst presidents of all time. For eight years, he presided over an economy that needs to be lied about to make it look like it is improving. Carson on the other hand is not only a brain surgeon; he is the best in his field. Carson relates to both blacks and whites, and he does not carry a race chip on his shoulder. Carson does not have to lie about anything. He is a model for us all.

Carson is the real deal, and he clearly knows enough about solutions that his formula for America's success that he brought forth at the Prayer Breakfast may very well elevate him one day to being one of the best President's America has ever seen. Wouldn't that be sweet? Meanwhile he is working hard to help make Donald Trump our next President.

At the very least, conservatives have found renewed hope that a fellow conservative with such high values actually does exist. In this world, which today offers few positive surprises, Ben Carson is a big one and a great one.

Like many of you, I had never heard of Dr. Ben Carson before February 7, 2013 when he addressed the National Prayer Breakfast. Among other dignitaries, President Barack Obama and first lady Michelle Obama were in attendance. Even the Obamas were brought found themselves standing as Carson put forth a speech that was almost as good as if Jesus himself had delivered it to the sinners and tax collectors of his time. And, yes, that is an intentional parallel. There were parables, biblical scriptures, and a lot of good humor and of course the good Doctor knocked it right out of the park.

Carson's message was that the country should use a common sense approach to issues such as freedom of speech, education, taxation, the national debt and spirituality. Without any indictment of President Obama, Carson produced a quiet to-do-list for the President. The only person in the room that day who could fill Carson's prescription for the renewed well-being of America was the President himself. Nonetheless Obama took the well-meaning advice as it was intended—as a gentleman. Unfortunately, after the event, there have been no press reports of Carson being invited to detail his views to the White House.

The First Lady was adding to the clamor with her applause at the end of the speech. It was as if she really did not realize that Dr. Carson's message was in direct conflict of everything her husband is doing to this country. Whether Obama eventually rejects Carson's message; he is ignoring it so far. Meanwhile, the American people are really digging it.

In 2013 when I wrote the first version of this book, it had already captured more than three million hits on YouTube and besides my own entreaties to the renowned surgeon, it has elicited headlines and many calls for more—such as the Wall Street Journal's "Ben Carson for President." Faith-based groups like the Pennsylvania Pastors' Network also gave Carson's remarks their blessings.

Sam Rohrer, president of the Pennsylvania Pastors' Network, and a past candidate for Governor in 2010 and for the US Senate in 2012 offered a profound summation of Carson's remarks:

"Dr. Carson verbalized sentiments felt but rarely voiced by a strong majority of American Christians who are committed to living according to the commands of scripture, Tenets like personal responsibility, moral uprightness, and fiscal restraint are not just smart politics; they are also biblically and constitutionally sound and the basis for America's success since its inception."

Wouldn't it be nice if Dr. Ben Carson became the first new American Party candidate for President when Trump finishes his second term?

Rather than tell you about the speech as it did go on for twenty-five minutes, I believe that the best way to introduce you all to Dr. Benjamin Carson is to let you listen to it yourself by doing an internet search for Dr. Ben Carson Prayer Breakfast where you may still read the full text of his speech. I provide a few paragraphs below just to whet your appetite.

Dr. Ben Carson's Speech at the 2013 National Prayer Breakfast

Posted on <u>February 13, 2013</u>   TRANSCRIPT VIA LYBIO.NET

[Benjamin Solomon "Ben" Carson, Sr. (September 18, 1951)]

"Thank you so much. Mr. President, Mr. Vice President, Mrs. Obama, distinguished guests – which included everybody. Thank you so much for this wonderful honor to be at this stage again. I was here 16 years ago, and the fact that they invited me back means that I didn't offend too many people, so that was great. [LAUGHTER]

I want to start by reading four texts which will put into I want to start by reading four texts which will put into context what I'm going to say.

Proverbs 11:9 With his mouth the Godless destroys his neighbor, but through knowledge the righteous escapes.

Proverbs 11:12 A man who lacks judgment derides his neighbor, but a man of understanding holds his tongue

Proverbs 11:25 A generous man will prosper. He who refreshes others will himself, be refreshed.
2nd Chronicles 7:14 If my people who are called by my name will humble themselves and pray and seek my face and turn from their wicked ways, then will I hear from heaven and will forgive their sins and heal their land.

You know, I have an opportunity to speak in a lot of venues. This is my fourth speech this week. And, I have an opportunity to talk to a lot of people. And I've been asking people what concerns you? What are you most concerned about in terms of the spirituality and the direction of our nation and our world? And I've talked to very prominent Democrats, very prominent Republicans. And I was surprised by the uniformity of their answers. And those have informed my comments this morning. Now, it's not my intention to offend anyone. I have discovered, however, in recent years that it's very difficult to speak to a large group of people these days and not offend someone. [laughter]

And people walk away with their feelings on their shoulders waiting for you to say something, ah, did you hear that? The PC police are out in force at all times. I remember once I was talking about the difference between a human brain and a dog's brain, and a man — and a dog, and a man got offended. You can't talk about dogs like that. [laughter] People focus in on that, completely miss the point of what you're saying. [laughter] And we've reached reach the point where people are afraid to actually talk about what they want to say because somebody might be offended. People are afraid to say Merry Christmas at Christmas time. Doesn't matter whether the person you're talking to is Jewish or, you know, whether they're any religion. That's a salutation, a greeting of goodwill. We've got to get over this sensitivity. You know, and it keeps people from saying what they really believe.

… "

…

My mother got married when she was 13. She was one of 24 children. She had a horrible life. She discovered that her husband was a bigamist, had another family. And she only had a third grade education. She had to take care of us. Dire poverty. I had a horrible temper, poor self-esteem. All the things that you think would preclude success.

But I had something very important. I had a mother who believed in me, and I had a mother who would never allow herself to be a victim no matter what happened.

She never made excuses, and she never accepted an excuse from us. And if we ever came up with an excuse, she always said do you have a brain? And if the answer was, yes, then she said then you could have thought your way out of it. It doesn't matter what John or Susan or Mary or anybody else did or said. And it was the most important thing she did for my brother and myself. Because if you don't accept excuses, pretty soon people stop giving them, and they start looking for solutions. And that is a critical issue when it comes to success.

Well, you know, we did live in dire poverty, and one of the things that I hated was poverty. You know, some people hate spiders, some people hate snakes, I hated poverty. I couldn't stand it. [laughter] But, you know, my mother couldn't stand the fact that we were doing poorly in school, and she prayed and asked god to give her wisdom, what could she do to – to make her sons understand the importance of wisdom? God gave her wisdom. At least in her opinion!

It was to turn off the TV, let us watch only two or three programs during the week, and read two books apiece and submit to her written book reports which she couldn't read—but we didn't know that.

...

Here's my solution. When a person is born, give him a birth certificate, an electronic medical record and a health savings account [HSA], to which money can be contributed, pre-tax from the time you are born, to the time you die. When you die, you can pass it on to your family members so that when you're 85 years old and you've got 6 diseases, you're not trying to spend up everything. You're happy to pass it on and nobody is talking about death panels. That's number one. Also –

Chapter Postface:

Several years ago, Dr. Carson released a new book titled, *America the Beautiful*, which is available at all the usual places. In this new book, Dr. Carson offers Americans a stark alternative to the vision President Barack Obama has put forth. Wouldn't it be nice if some time in the future, say eight years from now, he were President so he could implement his saving ideas for America?

AMERICA
the BEAUTIFUL

Rediscovering What Made This Nation Great

A *New York Times* Bestseller

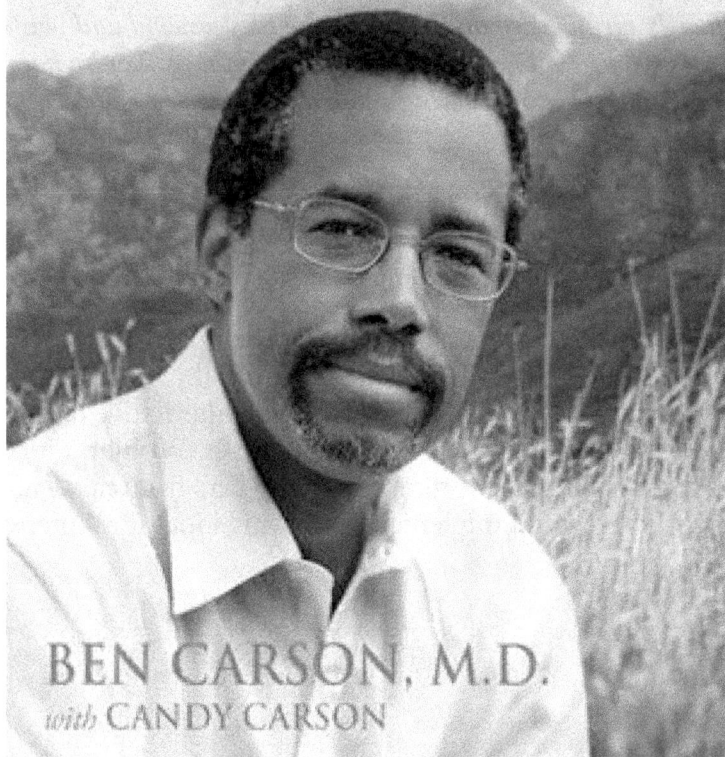

BEN CARSON, M.D.

with CANDY CARSON

Chapter 20

Republicans Stopped Defending American Exceptionalism

Democrats are the Enemy but Republicans Play Dead

This book asks conservatives to strongly consider saying good-by to the Republican Party by forming a party called the American Party and leaving the Republicans to swim in their own complacency. Conservatives and Tea Party people and populists and nationalists, who most often are one and the same, have a real enemy in the White House. His name as we well know is Barack Hussein Obama.

Obama favors Hillary Clinton as his replacement in chief. She would be just as bad if not worse. When I discuss Obama below, please consider Hillary having the same position. Remember both our President and his heir apparent are highly skilled liars. Both could outfox a fox.

Obama has never been just one person. He has so many liberal progressive minions in so many government agencies from the czars, to HUD to the EPA to Education, to Homeland Security etc. that if he were a good leader, he could command this army of loyalists into helping him take over the government all at once, rather than one Executive Order at a time.

Obama has already issued the command to change the country fundamentally a little at a time, and his pace has been quickening as he closes in on what should be the end of his second term. He has had to be somewhat concerned about moving too abruptly for if he were seen as being cocky with his power, it would have been a strategic mistake.

In the beginning of 2016, however his slow pace no longer seemed to matter. He engaged to get his will done as quickly as he could make thigs happen. And, of course there was always little publicity and even the Congress were often unaware of his shenanigans. Regardless of how far he gets on his agenda, in the next administration we must defeat him and all of his fascist and brainwashing propaganda and programs that he will leave behind in operational status.

This is not my first book about Obama and his plans to ruin America. I am the proud author of Kill the EPA! ; Obama's Seven Deadly Sins, and others. These are all available at www.bookhawkers.com, Amazon, and Kindle. You can get a real snoot-full on Obama in these books as well a number of other patriotic books at these sites.

There is a lot in this book about Obama, because, as I have said often, he is the ultimate enemy of every conservative who ever lived. This book clearly shows that the Republicans have not fought and continue not to fight Obama's most tyrannical moves. Republicans have abdicated their responsibilities as an opposition party. Obama is killing America and Republicans are playing dead!

Why is this book about Republicans instead of the Democratic leadership, the clear and continual enemy? The answer hit me like a ton of bricks. It was a wake-up call. All of a sudden, the GOP has chosen not to fight and not to help Americans fight the forces of evil taking over our country. They have control of both houses of Congress now yet they choose not to fight the many Obama messages and their armies of agencies.

There are two possibilities that I am evaluating. Republicans now seem to believe they have been dealt a winning hand in the Obama game or they are actually have been afraid of this

President for eight years. They seem to have the same fear of Hillary Clinton.

Either way, these are scary times for conservatives. Additionally, no reinforcements are coming any time soon from the establishment elitists of the Republican Party. In fact, many are abandoning their own party because Donald Trump has taken over by storm with full support of the non-elites and non-establishment members of the party and others outside the party who simply love America.

Jim Picht of the Washington Times offered a quick analysis of Republicans playing dead in his early January 2013 article about the fiscal cliff. Republicans have had big issues when dealing with what they obviously see as the fearsome Democrats for way too long. Conservatives have seen more than enough capitulation to expect anything to happen differently in the future.

Today, the opponents of Marxism and progressivism from all parties, including many Republicans believe the Republican establishment leadership ought to be ashamed of itself. Here is what Picht had to say in January 2013...

"**WASHINGTON,** DC, January 1, 2013 — Senate Minority Leader Mitch McConnell looked out over the fiscal cliff and, terrified, reached a compromise with the Obama Administration to avoid it.

"The compromise makes tax hikes for couples earning above $450,000 permanent; abandons the "chained CPI" calculation to slow entitlement growth; extends unemployment benefits for another year; raises estate, capital gains, and dividend taxes; extends tax benefits for education for five more years, and puts off sequestration for two months and pays for it with the new taxes. In return America gets $15 billion in spending cuts this year.

"This was a compromise the way that the Germans compromised with France in 1940, the way that the Redskins compromise with the Cowboys on Sundays. In his press conference Monday, President Obama crowed of this compromise, "You know, keep in mind that just last month, Republicans in Congress said they would never agree to raise tax rates on the wealthiest Americans. Obviously the agreement that's currently being discussed would raise those rates and raise them permanently." Obama was already gloating that he had killed the Republicans. Isn't it time that we conservatives simply put them out of their misery! They have been playing dead so long that when we kill the Party, nobody will notice?

For years, conservatives believed that the Republican Party values and conservative values were the same. Conservatives do not have their own Party, and for many years or so it seemed, Republicans were the enforcers for the conservative ideology. Conservatives thought Republicans felt the same as we do.

We all seemed to think during the Obama years that Democrats and their fascist president were ruining America. We all seemed concerned about what Obama could do in the short time left and what Hillary would do afterwards. Though it has been brewing for a while, Republicans during this period chose to no longer represent even themselves in dealing with Democrats. There is no fight left in the Republican Party.

Conservatives, which make up way more than 50% of the Republican Party and a substantial portion of all other parties could not afford to sit around until there was no America left to defend. We might joke about the prominence of Russia's Vladimir Putin in today's world as he might just be one leader worse than Obama. Yet, Obama is permitting him to gain strength at the expense of America's reputation. In the Economy and in foreign affairs, Obama has been trying to kill us and the Republicans have been pretending that "our day will come," without any pushback to the Obama agenda.

In this book, we unabashedly recommend to stop trusting Republicans since they have proven they will not fight for America or for conservative values. It is time for Trump. The leaders of the Grand Old Party have not even acknowledged that Obama and the Democrats have been wrong for eight years. Conservatives, Nationalists and Populists must go it alone.

The sooner conservatives cast off Republicans as our only protection against Democrats, the sooner we can move on to solving the problem for our values and our country. We need our own Party for sure; for without a Party, conservatives will not even be permitted on the battlefield when America is hanging by a thread.

Rush Limbaugh is a National Treasure

As I was putting the finishing touches on this book, and while I was making 24 quarts of V-6 juice today in the kitchen, I had the great pleasure of hearing the Rush Limbaugh Show on my big Radio. I think Rush Limbaugh is the smartest and most eloquent conservative spokesman. He is getting better every day. He sees all of the sinister attempts by Democrats and the corrupt press to bamboozle America and he has the guts to report on them.

Rush Limbaugh is a national treasure. I am not easily impressed but the newly invigorated Rush Limbaugh is the best asset America-loving Americans have. He is the best asset Americans have but many unfortunately are too stubborn and too brainwashed by liberal media to see it.

Since Obama became a force against America, Rush has been on our side as a true conservative and though he does not damn the Republican Party per se, he does damn their lack of action. When I originally wrote the first version of this book in 2013, Rush would not have advocated a dissolution of the Republican

Party in favor of an American Party. Now, I still am not sure but he might even help fund it.

Bush was not always right and in fact, he was often wrong. Of course, unlike Obama, Bush was not about ready to rip up the Constitution so he could become an irreplaceable power in the post Constitution years. Obama rips up a piece of the Constitution every day.

That is why conservatives fear him so much, especially when elite establishment Republicans just let him do it. Why Republicans fear him is another issue but I for one do not care about the reason anymore. I am finished with Republicans. You should be too.

I wish Rush Limbaugh would also say he is done with the Republican Party and then this book would not even have been necessary. Rush does everything but call for a new party yet he knows something must be put in place to fight the Democrats and he knows that it is not the new RINO Republican Party. That's why Rush is so favorable to Donald Trump. He wants anything but a Democrat in the White House, and the worst choice would be Hillary Clinton.

So, after making juice in the kitchen this morning, I began to listen at 12:06. I had a few more lines of tomatoes to crush for the juice. Rush was at his absolute best on this particular day.

Mr. Limbaugh talked about American Exceptionalism. We need this lecture every now and then. It was like hearing Paul Revere or George Washington or Thomas Jefferson explaining how the rest of the world from day one never experienced freedom. And Rush explains why our exceptionalism as a country stems back to the founders whose Constitution framed our entire government upon the fact that the people are in charge, not some outsiders, and not a bunch of friends that are known as the government.

Here are a few snippets from the September 12, 2013 program. In the first hour Limbaugh had taught a semester course in patriotism and why I want to be an American!

"So what is it? Well, if you know the history of the world... Read your Bible, read whatever historical account of humanity you hold dear, and what you'll read about is human tyranny. You'll read of bondage. You'll read of slavery. The vast majority of the people, the vast majority of the human beings who have lived and breathed and walked this planet have lived under the tyranny of despots, the vast majority. It isn't even close.

"The vast majority of the people of this world since the beginning of time have never known the kind of liberty and freedom that's taken for granted every day in this country. Most people have lived in abject fear of their leaders. Most people have lived in abject fear of whoever held power over them. Most people in the world have not had plentiful access to food and clean water. It was a major daily undertaking for most people to come up with just those two basic things.

"Just surviving was the primary occupation of most people in the world. The history of the world is dictatorship, tyranny, subjugation, whatever you want to call it of populations -- and then along came the United States of America. Pilgrims were the first to come here seeking freedom from all of that. They were oppressed because of their religion. They were told they had to believe in the king and his god, whatever it was, or they would be imprisoned.

"They led an exodus from Europe to this country, people of the same mind-set. They simply wanted to escape the tyranny of their ordinary lives. This country was founded that way. For the first time in human history, a government and country was founded on the belief that leaders serve the population. This country was the first in history, the EXCEPTION -- e-x-c-e-p-t, except. The exception to the rule is what American exceptionalism is.

"It is because of this liberty and freedom that our country exists, because the founders recognized it comes from God. It's part of the natural yearning of the human spirit. It is not granted by a government. It's not

granted by Putin. It's not granted by Obama or any other human being. We are created with the natural yearning to be free, and it is other men and leaders throughout human history who have suppressed that and imprisoned people for seeking it.

"The US is the first time in the history of the world where a government was organized with a Constitution laying out the rules, that the individual was supreme and dominant, and that is what led to the US becoming the greatest country ever because it unleashed people to be the best they could be. Nothing like it had ever happened. That's American exceptionalism. Putin doesn't know what it is, Obama doesn't know what it is, and it just got trashed in the New York Times. It's just unacceptable."

I ask you to take your time but when you have the time, read the full text of this. Rush is a great teacher. It will help you understand that many Americans take the freedom of our country for granted because they have known nothing else. America is an exceptional country and if Republicans are not willing to fight for this country, then it is time for conservatives and Nationalists and Populists to join together, with Rush Limbaugh's help to get this big job done.

Kill the Republican Party and then immediately Bring on the American Party! Thank you for being with me in this book. God bless you and of course may God bless the United States of America.

This is great. Thanks Rush. ?

LETS GO PUBLISH! Books by Brian Kelly:
(sold at www.bookhawkers.com Amazon.com, and Kindle.).

LETS GO PUBLISH! is proud to announce that more AS/400 and Power i books are becoming available to help you inexpensively address your AS/400 and Power i education and training needs: Our general titles precede specific AS/400 and other technology books.

Why Trump?
You Already Know... But, this book will tell you anyway

Saving America The Trump Way!
A book that tells you how President Donald Trump will help Merica dn Americans wind up on top

The US Immigration Fix
It's all in here. You won't want to put it down

Great Moments in Penn State Football Check out the particulars of this great book at bookhawkers.com.

Great Moments in Notre Dame Football Check out the particulars of this great book at bookhawkers.com or www.notredamebooks.com

WineDiets.Com Presents The Wine Diet Learn how to lose weight while having fun. Four specific diets and some great anecdotes fill this book with fun and the opportunity to lose weight in the process.

Wilkes-Barre, PA; Return to Glory Wilkes-Barre City's return to glory begins with dreams and ideas. Along with plans and actions, this equals leadership.

The Lifetime Guest Plan. This is a plan which if deployed today would immediately solve the problem of 60 million illegal aliens in the United States.

Geoffrey Parsons' Epoch... The Land of Fair Play Better than the original. The greatest re-mastering of the greatest book ever written on American Civics. It was built for all Americans as the best govt. design in the history of the world.

The Bill of Rights 4 Dummmies! This is the best book to learn about your rights. Be the first, to have a "Rights Fest" on your block. You will win for sure!

Sol Bloom's Epoch ...Story of the Constitution This work by Sol Bloom was written to commemorate the Sesquicentennial celebration of the Constitution. It has been remastered by Lets Go Publish! – An excellent read!

The Constitution 4 Dummmies! This is the best book to learn about the Constitution. Learn all about the fundamental laws of America.

America for Dummmies!
All Americans should read to learn about this great country.

Just Say No to Chris Christie for President!
Discusses the reasons why Chris Christie is a poor choice for US President

The Federalist Papers by Hamilton, Jay, Madison w/ intro by Brian Kelly
Complete unabridged, easier to read version of the original Federalist Papers

Kill the Republican Party!
Demonstrates why the Republican Party must be abandoned by conservatives

Bring On the American Party!
Demonstrates how conservatives can be free from the party of wimps by starting its own national party called the American Party.

No Amnesty! No Way!
In addition to describing the issue in detail, this book also offers a real solution.

Saving America
This how-to book is about saving our country using strong mercantilist principles. These same principles that helped the country from its founding.

RRR:
A unique plan for economic recovery and job creation

Kill the EPA
The EPA seems to hate mankind and love nature. They are also making it tough for asthmatics to breathe and for those with malaria to live. It's time they go.

Obama's Seven Deadly Sins.
In the Obama Presidency, there are many concerns about the long-term prospects and sustainability of the country. We examine each of the President's seven deadliest sins in detail, offering warnings and a number of solutions. Be careful. Book may nudge you to move to Canada or Europe.

Taxation Without Representation Second Edition
At the time of the Boston Tea Party, there was no representation. Now, there is no representation again but there are "representatives."

Healthcare Accountability
Who should pay for your healthcare? Whose healthcare should you pay for? Is it a lifetime free ride on others or should those once in need of help have to pay it back when their lives improve?

Jobs! Jobs! Jobs!
Where have all the American Jobs gone and how can we get them back?

Other IBM I Technical Books

The All Everything Operating System:
Story about IBM's finest operating system; its facilities; how it came to be.

The All-Everything Machine
Story about IBM's finest computer server.

Chip Wars
The story of ongoing wars between Intel and AMD and upcoming wars between Intel and IBM. Book may cause you to buy / sell somebody's stock.

Can the AS/400 Survive IBM?
Exciting book about the AS/400 in a System i5 World.

The IBM i Pocket SQL Guide.
Complete Pocket Guide to SQL as implemented on System i5. A must have for SQL developers new to System i5. It is very compact yet very comprehensive and it is example driven. Written in a part tutorial and part reference style, Tons of SQL coding samples, from the simple to the sublime.

The IBM i Pocket Query Guide.
If you have been spending money for years educating your Query users, and you find you are still spending, or you've given up, this book is right for you. This one QuikCourse covers all Query options.

The IBM I Pocket RPG & RPG IV Guide.
Comprehensive RPG & RPGIV Textbook -- Over 900 pages. This is the one RPG book to have if you are not having more than one. All areas of the language covered smartly in a convenient sized book Annotated PowerPoint's available for self-study (extra fee for self-study package)

The IBM I RPG Tutorial and Lab Guide – Recently Revised.
Your guide to a hands-on Lab experience. Contains CD with Lab exercises and PowerPoint's. Great companion to the above textbook or can be used as a standalone for student Labs or tutorial purposes

The IBM i Pocket Developers' Guide.
Comprehensive Pocket Guide to all of the AS/400 and System i5 development tools - DFU, SDA, etc. You'll also get a big bonus with chapters on Architecture, Work Management, and Subfile Coding.

The IBM i Pocket Database Guide.
Complete Pocket Guide to System i5 integrated relational database (DB2/400) – physical and logical files and DB operations - Union, Projection, Join, etc. Written in a part tutorial and part reference style. Tons of DDS coding samples.

Getting Started with The WebSphere Development Studio Client for System i5 (WDSc).
Focus is on client server and the Web. Includes CODE/400, VisualAge RPG, CGI, WebFacing, and WebSphere Studio. Case study continues from the Interactive Book.

The System i5 Pocket WebFacing Primer.
This book gets you started immediately with WebFacing. A sample case study is used as the basis for a conversion to WebFacing. Interactive 5250 application is WebFaced in a case study form before your eyes.

Getting Started with WebSphere Express Server for IBM i Step-by-Step Guide for Setting up Express Servers
A comprehensive guide to setting up and using WebSphere Express. It is filled with examples, and structured in a tutorial fashion for easy learning.

The WebFacing Application Design & Development Guide:
Step by Step Guide to designing green screen IBM i apps for the Web. Both a systems design guide and a developers guide. Book helps you understand how to design and develop Web applications using regular RPG or COBOL programs.

The System i5 Express Web Implementer's Guide.
Your one stop guide to ordering, installing, fixing, configuring, and using WebSphere Express, Apache, WebFacing, System i5 Access for Web, and HATS/LE.

Joomla! Technical Books

Best Damn Joomla Tutorial Ever
Learn Joomla! By example.

Best Damn Joomla Intranet Tutorial Ever
This book is the only book that shows you how to use Joomla on a corporate intranet.

Best Damn Joomla Template Tutorial Ever
This book teaches you step-by step how to work with templates in Joomla!

Best Damn Joomla Installation Guide Ever
Teaches you how to install Joomla! On all major platforms besides IBM i.

Best Damn Blueprint for Building Your Own Corporate Intranet.
This excellent timeless book helps you design a corporate intranet for any platform while using Joomla as its basis.
4
IBM i PHP & MySQL Installation & Operations Guide
How to install and operate Joomla! on the IBM i Platform

IBM i PHP & MySQL Programmers Guide
programs for IBM i

www.ingramcontent.com/pod-product-compliance
Lightning Source LLC
Chambersburg PA
CBHW072130270326
41931CB00010B/1720